COLLOQUIAL
FRENCH

THE COLLOQUIAL SERIES

*Colloquial Albanian
*Colloquial Arabic (Levantine)
*Colloquial Arabic of Egypt
*Colloquial Arabic of the Gulf and Saudi Arabia
*Colloquial Chinese
*Colloquial Dutch
*Colloquial English
*Colloquial French
 Colloquial German
 Colloquial Greek
*Colloquial Hungarian
*Colloquial Italian
*Colloquial Japanese
*Colloquial Persian
*Colloquial Polish
 Colloquial Portuguese
*Colloquial Romanian
 Colloquial Russian
*Colloquial Serbo-Croat
 Colloquial Spanish
*Colloquial Swedish
*Colloquial Turkish

*Accompanying cassette available

COLLOQUIAL
FRENCH

R. A. Humphreys

London and New York

TO JANE, MY WIFE,
FOR ALL HER HELP AND PATIENCE

First published in 1980
by Routledge & Kegan Paul
Reprinted in 1991 and 1992
by Routledge
11 New Fetter Lane, London EC4P 4EE

Simultaneously published in the USA and Canada by Routledge
a division of Routledge, Chapman and Hall, Inc.
29 West 35th Street, New York, NY 10001

© R. A. Humphreys 1980

Set in 9 on 11pt. Linotron Times, by
Rowland Phototypesetting Ltd, Bury St Edmunds, Suffolk
and printed in Great Britain by
Cox & Wyman Ltd, Reading

British Library Cataloguing in Publication Data

Humphreys, R.A.
Colloquial French. – (Colloquial Series).
1. French language – Conversation and
phrase books
2. French language — Spoken French
I. Title
448'.3'421   PC2121   80–40688

ISBN 0415–03945–2 (paperback)
ISBN 0415–03889–8 (cassette)
ISBN 0415–03890–1 (book and cassette course pack)

CONTENTS

PART TWO   READING PASSAGES AND VOCABULARY

INTRODUCTION

'Colloquial' is defined by the *Shorter Oxford English Dictionary* as 'belonging to common speech or ordinary conversation'; French is a language spoken by millions of people all over the world.

Colloquial French is intended for four broad groups of people: (1) those meeting French for the first time and who need rapidly to acquire basic conversational competence, (2) those who have forgotten the French they once knew and now wish to rebuild on old groundwork, (3) young people facing examinations and needing a short but comprehensive revision of first principles, (4) travellers of all ages who require a practical guide to the language of France.

The book sets out to give the reader examples of the kind of 'common speech' likely to be directed at him or her by French people in the normal course of everyday life in France and aims to provide a basic stock of grammar, vocabulary and idiom with which to carry on 'ordinary conversation' in French.

'Common speech' is not a lazy alternative to 'speaking properly'; nor does it consist of a string of picturesque but dislocated colloquialisms. It is the language of ordinary people and demands as much accuracy as formal speech.

Part I of this book begins by introducing the sounds and some aspects of the behaviour which make up 'common speech' in French. I have tried to emphasise the fundamental importance of pronunciation and to explain it in a readily comprehensible fashion.

It then continues with twenty 'lessons' systematically covering the grammatical structure of the language. Points of grammar are introduced, tested by exercises and illustrated by examples drawn from everyday spoken French. The lessons contain conversational material designed to help the reader in common practical situations. 'Ordinary conversation' is fluid, not stereotyped; however, I have tried to cover the vocabulary and expressions most likely to occur in each given situation.

Lesson nineteen is meant as a brief introduction to the vast body of 'slang' terminology which is an essential part of spoken French. Treat it with care!

Part II contains three connected passages of prose for analysis; each illustrates how 'common speech' can be an effective literary form. To conclude this section, there is a short selection of maxims and poems for translation and appreciation.

Finally, I have provided an English-French vocabulary as a last resort for when, at the critical moment, memory fails.

Having worked through this book, the reader will have laid a foundation; constant effort and practice, where possible, will be needed to maintain, adjust and build on that foundation. It is a difficult but constantly rewarding task to understand and contribute to the 'common speech or ordinary conversation' of the French.

A cassette has been produced to accompany this book so that the student can hear French spoken by native speakers. All material recorded on the cassette is marked by a ■ in the text.

PART ONE

■ PRONUNCIATION

A good pronunciation is the most important thing you can learn in French. Without it, all the grammar, vocabulary and idiom you know will be nothing but a meaningless jumble of unfamiliar sounds to a French person.

Imagine you're at Dover docks waiting for a ferry, when a foreigner comes up to you, gesticulating in that wild Latin way, and asks excitedly: 'Excuse me, weirdos, these sheep go too?' No one would blame you for shaking your head and muttering something about excitable Frenchmen. In fact, of course, he was saying: 'Excuse me, where does this ship go to?' but it was all gibberish to you, because he made the sounds strangely and got the intonation wrong.

In the reverse situation, we are much more easily misunderstood by the Frenchman because his vowel-sounds are more precise and his intonation pattern is different. Consider the following:

ÇA   SON   C'EST   SI   SOUS   SOIE   SUIS   CE   SOT   SU

These are ten different words consisting of S + vowel, but each word has a different meaning. To speak French comprehensibly, your vowel-sounds must be accurate.

There's no escaping the fact that learning to speak French 'like a Frenchman' is very difficult. Unless you spend some time in France, all you can do is to make a point of listening to the radio regularly, even if at first you don't understand what is being said. But the more you listen, the more will seem familiar. The further you progress through this book, the more you will understand of what you hear on the radio.

Start as you mean to go on – make sure you get the sound right!

■ VOWELS

In French, vowels are pronounced more intensely, more purely, than in English. There is none of the slurring or drawling of vowels which particularly characterises southern English.

Here are the eleven French vowel sounds and the symbols used in this book to represent them:

Symbol	English equivalent	Written as	Examples
a	*a*n, b*a*nd, c*a*t	a, ea, e+mm	l*a*, ç*a*, mang*ea*, f*emm*e
A	*a*rt, f*a*rm, f*a*ther	â, a+silent (s)	*â*me, p*â*le, b*a*s, t*a*s
é	l*a*te, *ai*d (pronounced sharply)	é, ez, final ai, final er	parl*é*, n*ez*, j'*ai*, aim*er*
E	*ai*r, b*ea*r, st*a*re	è, ê, ei, ai e+most consonants	p*è*re, bl*ê*me, p*ei*ne, *ai*ment, s*e*l
i	sh*ee*p, mach*i*ne	i, î, y	v*i*lle, d*î*ner, st*y*le
o	somewhere between b*o*ne and b*u*n	o + sounded consonant	n*o*te, d*o*nne, m*o*de
O	s*o*, p*o*le, l*oa*d	o, ô, au, eau	n*o*s, dr*ô*le, ch*au*d, chap*eau*
OO	st*oo*l, c*oo*l	ou, où, aoû	f*ou*, j*ou*r, *où*, g*oû*t, a*oû*t
U	Scots 'g*ui*d' (good)	u, û, eu	*u*sage, s*û*r, *u*ni, t*u*, j'ai *eu*
œ	b*u*rn, l*u*rk, sh*i*rt	eu, oeu	d*eu*x, *Eu*rope
e	di*e*t, qui*e*t, fin*a*l	e in mono-syllables or first syllable	l*e*, m*e*, r*e*garder, b*e*soin

■ SEMI-VOWELS

These sounds are always combined with another vowel.

| Y | yawn, say, lay | y, i, ll (+ vowel) | yeux, pied, bibliothèque, vieille |
| W | west, wee, worth | ou, oi (+ vowel) | oui, ouest, moi, loi |

Note: U is a sound which is not used in English. Say 'ee' as in sheep and while making the sound, round your lips to the shape of an 'o'. The resulting sound is like the Scots pronunciation of 'guid'.

Practise the distinction between U and OO:

su – sous.

An *e* at the end of a word is silent and the sound 'e' in the middle of a word is glossed over. Eg: phare (FaR), porte (PoRT), petite (PTiT), matelot (MaTLO).

▮ NASAL VOWELS

Nasal vowels do not exist in English. The nearest equivalent is the sound in song, fang, without the 'g'. The French sounds are Ē, Ā, Ō, œ̄, pronounced while breathing through the mouth and nose at the same time.

Ē	mangle	in, im, ain, aim, ein, ien	fin, simple, main, faim, bien, dessein
Ā	thong	am, an, em, en, ean	champ, banc, emporter, ennui, vengeance
Ō	norm	on om	non, son, nom, plomb
œ̄	bung	un, um	aucun, brun, parfum

Practise the distinction between Ē, Ā, Ō, œ̄:

main – mansarde – mon – parfum;
bain – banc – bon – album.

■ CONSONANTS

Symbol	English equivalent	Written as	Examples
P	*p*lace, car*p*	p, pp	*p*eau, ap*p*orter
B	*b*lood, cu*b*	b, bb	*b*leu, a*bb*é
F	*f*lute, cu*ff*	f, ph	*f*ou, *ph*ysique
V	*v*ision, co*v*er	v, w	cou*v*re, *w*agon
T	*t*rain, ra*t*e	t, tt, th	*t*uile, ne*tt*e, *th*éologie
D	*d*rone, toa*d*	d, dd	*d*onne, ad*d*ition
K	*c*oat, la*ck*	q, c (+ a, o, u), k, qu, ch	co*q*, *c*ouler, *k*ilo, *qu*e, é*ch*o
G	*g*one, la*g*	g (+ a, o), gu	*g*ant, *gu*êpe
S	*s*ong, ba*ss*	s, sc, ss, t (+ i), c (+ e, i), ç (+ a, o, u)	*sc*ience, ma*ss*e, ac*t*ion, *s*ang, *c*es, gar*ç*on
Z	*z*oo, fro*z*e	z, s (between vowels)	*z*èle, ra*s*er, ca*s*er
ZH	lei*s*ure, plea*s*ure	j, g (+ i, e)	*j*e, lo*g*e, sta*g*e, *j*our
SH	sma*sh*, *sh*oe	ch, sh	*ch*ou, *ch*amp, *sh*ort
R	(see below)	r, rr	*r*ang, co*rr*uption
M	*m*ime, le*m*on	m, mm	*m*ère, com*m*un
N	*n*aughty, *n*one	n, nn	*n*ous, son*n*er
L	*l*uck, coo*l*	l, ll	*l*ourd, co*ll*er
NY	*n*ew, *n*ude	gn	a*gn*eau, bai*gn*er
KS	a*x*e, la*x*	x	a*x*e, *x*ylophone

English people often find the French 'r' a major stumbling-block, but there is really no reason why they should. There are two ways of pronouncing it. In Northern France, the sound is made at the back of the throat, with a vibration of the tonsils. The best way to master this is to copy the French singer Edith Piaf singing 'Non, je ne *regrette rien*'. In the South, 'r' is trilled, at the front of the mouth, like a Scots 'r'. Either way is perfectably acceptable, and it is less important to perfect what is called 'the French *r*' than it is to distinguish clearly between your vowel sounds.

Consonants at the end of words are usually silent, except K, F, L, R:

so: champ = SHÃ   banc = BÃ   sot = SO   las = La
but: fac = FaK   prof = PRoF   col = KoL   bar = BaR

All final consonants would be sounded in liaison.

The letter 'h' has no sound in French. Where 'h' begins a word, however, in some cases it is aspirated. This means that, although it has no sound, it acts as a blockage – a mental pause – between two words, which prevents the normal contraction from *le* or *la* to *l'* being made. Other words begin with a mute *h* and with these words the contraction *l'* is made:

aspirate: la*hache, le*hameau, le*homard
mute: l'hôtel, l'homme

■ ACCENTS

There are three written accents – the acute (´), the grave (`) and the circumflex (ˆ).

The circumflex usually indicates that the vowel is long. Contrast the sound in *tache* (TaSH) with *tâche* (TASH), *lache* (LaSH) with *lâche* (LASH).

The acute and grave accents are used to differentiate between the sounds é and E. Contrast *pétiller* (PéTiYé) with *père* (PER).

Two other written signs are used:

(¸), the cedilla, is written under a *c* to indicate a soft 's' sound, rather than a hard 'k'. Contrast *garçon* (GaRSŌ) with *flacon* (FLaKŌ).

(¨), the diaeresis, shows that two vowels are pronounced separately, not as a diphthong: *noël* (NOEL) and *naïf* (NaiF).

Look carefully at the vowel chart to see how these accents and signs affect pronunciation.

■ LIAISON

The final consonant of a word is usually silent. But when the first letter of the following word is a vowel or *h* mute, then that preceding consonant is sounded. Thus liaison involves running two words together:

tou*t* à fait (TOOTaFé)   es*t*-il? (éTiL?)

In liaison, *s* and *x* are sounded as Z, *d* as T, and *f* as V:

le*s* avions (LéZaVYŌ)   vieu*x* hommes (VYeZoM)
gran*d* éclat (GRĀTéKLa)   neu*f* ans (NœVĀ)

Liaison is never made with *et* (and), and always made with *trop* (too much). Its use is obligatory between article and noun, but elsewhere, tends to sound rather formal. It is becoming increasingly less common in colloquial speech.

■ ELISION

The final *e* in some monosyllables is elided before a word beginning with a vowel or mute *h*: de – d', le – l', me – m', que – qu'.

qu'est-ce? d'autres m'appelle

In speech, groups of words are run together; so much so that short words are often left out. *Ne* is frequently omitted:

je ne suis pas (ZHSWiPa)
je ne sais pas (ZHSéPa)
tu ne crois pas (TKRWaPa)
ce n'est pas important (SPaĒPoRTĀ)

In speech, but not in writing, *tu* is frequently elided to *t'*: tu as = t'as.

■ STRESS AND INTONATION

The final syllable of English words is rarely stressed. We say:

*camp*ing, *go*vernment, ad*vent*ure, im*poss*ible

The syllables of French words are much more evenly stressed, but what stress there is usually falls on the last syllable. A word given the wrong stress may be incomprehensible. Practise stressing the last syllable in these examples:

camping (KĀPiNY) gouvernement (GOOVERNeMĀ)
aventure (aVĀTUR) impossible (ĒPoSiBL)

Each group of words also has a distinct intonation.

In a statement, the intonation rises at the end of each breath-group and falls at the end of the sentence:

_____/ _____/ _____/ ‾‾‾‾\ .

In a question, the intonation rises:

_____/ _____/ _____/?

In an imperative, the intonation falls and the word expressing the order is stressed:

————— !
——

Many words of Anglo-American origin are commonly used in French, but their pronunciation and often their meaning has become modified. Practise saying the following words out loud:

le shopping (LeSHoPiNY) –	window-shopping, expensive shopping
le smoking (LeSMoKiNY) –	dinner-jacket
le shampooing (LeSHĀPWĒ) –	shampoo
le camping (LeKĀPiNY) –	camping, camping site
le parking (LePaRKiNY) –	car-park, parking lot
le jogging (LeZHoGiNY) –	jogging
le building (Le BiLDiNY) –	multi-storey building
le gas-oil (LeGaZWaL) –	diesel
le whisky soda (LeWiSKiSoDa) –	whisky and soda
les rugbymen (LéRUGBiMEN) –	rugby players
le western (LeWESTERN) –	western film, cowboys and Indians
le sex-appeal (LeSEKSaPiL) –	sex-appeal, charm
les girls (LéGœRL) –	show-girls, dancers
le week-end (Le WiKEND) –	weekend
le super (LeSUPER) –	high octane petrol
le recordman (LeREKoRDMaN) –	record-holder
le gangster (LeGĀSTER) –	robber, villain
le shakehand (LeSHéKaND) –	handshake
le short (LeSHoRT) –	short trousers

SPELLING

An analysis of French spelling is outside the scope of a book entitled *Colloquial French*. However, two points are worth mentioning.

First, *je* (meaning 'I') is spelled with an initial capital letter only when it begins a sentence.

Second, adjectives of nationality are spelled without a capital letter; for example, *la vie bohème* (LaViBOEM) and *le franc français* (LeFRĀFRĀSé).

BEHAVIOUR

Learning a language not only involves learning words and constructions, but also the social customs which that language reflects. However little French you can actually speak, you will feel much more at home in France once you are familiar with how the French behave to each other.

■ GREETINGS

Bonjour (BŌZHOOR) Hello/Good morning/ Good day	Monsieur (MSYe) Sir	Messieurs (MéSYe) Gentlemen
Bonsoir (BŌSWAR) Good evening/Good night	Madame (MaDaM) Madam	Mesdames (MéDaM) Ladies
Au revoir (ORVWAR) Good-bye	Mademoiselle (MaDMWAZEL) Miss	Mesdemoiselles MéDMWAZEL) (single) Ladies

To be polite, you must use the greeting and an appropriate title together:

Bonjour, Madame, Monsieur. Mesdames, Mesdemoiselles, au revoir.

When they enter a room, French people acknowledge everyone present, whether or not they have met them before. For example, anyone coming into a small shop or bar will greet the person serving and any other customers, saying, 'Mesdames et Messieurs, bonjour', or, more commonly, 'Bonjour, Messieurs Dames', and will often shake hands with everyone. Similarly, on leaving, a French person will usually shake hands again. To fail to express the customary courtesies may be regarded as a sign of bad manners or surliness:

Je vous présente Monsieur X (ZHVOOPRéZÊT) – Let me introduce you to Mr X
Enchanté de faire votre connaissance (ÊSHÊTéDeFER VOTRKoNESÊS) – Pleased to meet you

When speaking to friends and acquaintances, a less formal manner should be used:

Salut (SaLU) – Hi!
Salut, mon vieux (MŌVYe) – Hello, mate, old chap
Salut, les gars (LéGaR) – Hello lads
À bientôt (aBYĒTO) – Bye, see you soon.
À tout à l'heure (ATOOTaLœ R) – See you later
À la prochaine (aLaPRoSHEN) – Till next time
À demain (aDeMÃ) – See you tomorrow
À ce soir (aSeSWAR) – See you this evening
À un de ces jours, peut-être (aœ DSéZHOOR PTETR) – See you again, perhaps
Adieu (ADYe) – Good-bye

With all forms of leave-taking, *Allez* (aLé) – Right, well, OK, is often used: Allez, à bientôt. Allez, au revoir, Madame. Allez, à la prochaine.

Bonjour, *Bonsoir*, *Salut* and *Adieu* can mean both Hello and Good-bye.

Bonne nuit (BoNWi) means 'Good night', but is said only to someone who is actually going to bed.

■ OTHER FORMS OF ADDRESS

Whatever you are doing, French people will wish you well. They may say:

Bonne route (BoNROOT) – Have a good journey
Bon voyage (BŌNWaYAZH) – Have a good trip
Bonne continuation (BoNKŌTiNUaSYŌ) – Good luck with the rest of your trip; I hope all turns out well
Bon appétit (BŌNaPéTi) – Have a good meal
Bonne chance (BoNSHÃS) – Good luck
Attention! (aTĒSYŌ) – Look out!

■ ACCEPTING, REFUSING, THANKING, EXCUSING

If you are offered something you wish to accept, then say:

Je veux bien (ZHVeBYĒ) (or) Oui, merci (WiMERSi) (or)

Volontiers (VoLÕTYé) (or) Je vous remercie (or) Avec plaisir (aVEKPLéZiR), all of which mean 'With pleasure'.
'Merci' in reply to an offer means 'No thank you'. Otherwise it means 'Thank you'.
The reply then is:
'De rien' (DeRYÊ), (or) 'Il n'y a pas de quoi' (YaPaDKWa) – 'Thank you, not at all'.
'Pardon' (PaRDÕ) (and) 'Excusez-moi' (EKSKUZéMWA) both mean 'Pardon', 'Excuse me'. The reply to this is 'Je vous en prie' (ZHVOOÃPRI) – 'Certainly'.
Je regrette, mais . . . (ZHe ReGRETMé) – I'm sorry, but . . .

TU and VOUS, casual and polite

Both *tu* (TU) and *vous* (VOO) mean you.

Vous is the plural form and is used to refer to more than one person. It is also the polite form of 'you' (singular). As a general rule it should be used when you are speaking to people you don't know, to most people older than you are, to all officials and to anyone else you feel you should be polite to.

Tu is the casual form of 'you' (singular). Friends, students, anyone dressed casually and people under thirty who seem cheerful or friendly should be called *tu*.

However, be very careful about which form you use, because to call someone *tu* who should be called *vous* is very rude, while to call someone *vous* who should be called *tu* will seem standoffish or unfriendly. The only thing you can do is to listen carefully and discover what you yourself are being called; then you can adopt the same form. But listen carefully, because after a short while the Frenchman may change to *tu*, if he's getting on well with you, or alternatively change from *tu* to *vous* if he decides he doesn't like you.

Tu is also the form to use when you want to be very offensive.

LESSON ONE

GENDER

English nouns have no gender. Some people, such as boys and girls, are obviously male or female, while others, such as teachers and drivers, could be either.

Things such as houses, books and aeroplanes are neither male nor female. By convention, a few things are given gender. For example, a ship is always referred to as 'she' although there is nothing female about ships.

French nouns have gender. By convention, they are all either masculine or feminine. In most cases, the gender of a noun is not related to its meaning. In French, books are masculine and houses are feminine, by grammatical convention. But in a few obvious cases, the meaning of a noun dictates its gender:

Masc.	Fem.
l'homme – man	la femme – woman, wife
le père – father	la mère – mother
le grand-père – grandfather	la grand'mère – grandmother
le frère – brother	la soeur – sister
le fils – son	la fille – daughter, girl
l'oncle – uncle	la tante – aunt
le garçon – boy	la fiancée – fiancee
le mari ⎫ l'époux ⎬ – husband	l'épouse – wife
le neveu – nephew	la nièce – niece
l'ami – friend (male)	l'amie – friend (female)
le copain – mate, chum	la copine – chum (female)
le cousin – cousin (male)	la cousine – cousin (female)
le veuf – widower	la veuve – widow
le célibataire – bachelor	la célibataire – spinster
le gosse – kid (male)	la gosse – kid (female)
le gamin – kid, youngster (male)	la gamine – kid, youngster (female)
le paysan – peasant, yokel	la paysanne – peasant woman
le type – bloke	la nana – bird (= girl)

le bébé means a baby, whether boy or girl
l'enfant means a child, whether male or female
les parents is masc. plural and means parents or relations

How can we tell whether a noun is masculine or feminine?

THE ARTICLE

The article is a sign of gender. Its form changes to agree with the gender of the noun it refers to. When you meet a noun for the first time, always learn it with the appropriate article, and then you will be sure of its gender.

The definite article – le, la, l', les

Masc. sing.	le –	le livre – the book
	l' –	l'avion – the aeroplane
Fem. sing.	la –	la maison – the house
	l' –	l'ombre – the shadow

Both *le* and *la* contract to *l'* before a vowel or *h* mute.

Plural	les –	les livres – the books
		les avions – the aeroplanes
		les maisons – the houses
		les ombres – the shadows

Distinguish clearly between *le* and *la*. The wrong sound may give the wrong meaning. *Le* livre = the book, but *la* livre = the pound (weight) or the pound (sterling). Quite a difference!

The indefinite article

Masc. sing.	un –	un livre – a book
Fem. sing.	une –	une ombre – a shadow
Plural	des –	des avions – aeroplanes, some aeroplanes
		des ombres – shadows, some shadows
		des maisons – houses, some houses

L' can signify either gender, so learn nouns beginning with a vowel or *h* mute with the indefinite article.

NUMBER

The plural of most nouns is formed by adding *s* to the singular:

livres, maisons, avions, ombres

The *s* is silent, except in liaison where it is pronounced Z. Since there is normally no difference in sound between singular and plural (homme, hommes), the important number sign is the article (*l*'homme, *les* hommes).

However, some nouns form their plurals irregularly. Those ending in *s*, *x* and *z* are unchanged in the plural:

la souris – mouse; la voix – voice; le nez – nose

Those ending in *al* and *ail* usually change to *aux*:

le cheval, les chevaux – horse(s)
le journal, les journaux – newspaper(s)
le travail, les travaux – work(s)
le canal, les canaux – canal(s)

Those ending in *eu* and *eau* add *x* in the plural:

le feu, les feux – fire
une eau, des eaux – water
le cheveu, les cheveux – hair

The following seven nouns ending in *ou* add *x* in the plural:

le bijou – jewel   le hibou – owl
le caillou – pebble   le joujou – toy
le chou – cabbage   le pou – louse
le genou – knee

Three oddities are:

un oeil (ŪNoeY) – eye   des yeux (DéZYoe) – eyes
un os (ŪNoS) – bone   des os (DéZO) – bones
un oeuf (ŪNoeF) – egg   des oeufs (DéZoe) – eggs

DE (of, from)

le livre de Martin – Martin's book (the book of Martin)
un kilomètre de Paris – a (one) kilometre from Paris
le journal d'Henri – Henry's paper (the paper of Henry)

The English 's denoting possession does not exist in French. Before a vowel or *h* mute, *de* contracts to *d'*.

À (in, at, to)

à la maison – at home, in the house
à Londres – in or to London
de and *à* with the definite article:

de + le = du	à + le = au
de + la = de la	à + la = à la
de + l' = de l'	à + l' = à l'
de + les = des	à + les = aux

Examples

au milieu du jardin – in the middle of the garden
au centre de la ville – in the centre of the town
à l'intérieur de l'appartement (m) – in the inside of the flat
l'extérieur (m) du mur – the outside of the wall
au milieu du plancher – in the middle of the floor
à la sortie de l'usine (f) – at the factory exit
à l'entrée (f) de la banque – at the entrance to the bank
aux environs de Londres – on the outskirts of London
au bout d'un moment – after a moment

jusqu'à (until, up to) changes in the same way as *à*:

aller jusqu'à Toulouse – to go as far as Toulouse
aller jusqu'au bout – to go right to the end
du matin jusqu'au soir – from morn(ing) to night
jusqu'au dernier moment – up to the last moment
jusqu'à quand? – until when?
jusqu'à aujourd'hui – until today
jusqu'à maintenant – up until now

■ DIRECTIONS

où est . . . ? – where is . . . ?
au coin de la rue – at the corner of the street
près de la boutique – near the (small) shop
au bord du trottoir – on the kerb (edge of the pavement)

à côté de l'Hôtel (m) de Ville – near (next to) the Town Hall
en face de l'immeuble (m) – opposite the building (block of flats)
devant l'église (f) – in front of the church
derrière le parking – behind the car park
sous le pont – under the bridge
au fond de la salle – at the end (back) of the room
attention à la voiture! – watch out for the car!
au travail – at work
au garage – in the garage
au soleil – in the sunshine
aller à pied – to go on foot
au loin, au lointain – in the distance
à gauche et à droite – on the left and on the right
aller tout droit – to go straight on
sur la route de Paris – on the road to Paris
sur la place Pigalle – in Pigalle Square
dans la rue Henri IV – in Henry IV Street

■ *Pronunciation*

U – s*u*r, *u*sine, voit*u*re, d*u*, r*u*e, m*u*r, *u*ne, aven*u*e
O – *eau*x, chev*au*x, côté, des *o*s, *au*
Ã – dev*an*t, *en*, c*en*tre, *en*trée, b*an*que, mom*en*t
 Õ – p*on*t, f*on*d, envir*on*s, L*on*dres, *om*bres
 Yoe – mil*ieu*, intér*ieu*r, *yeu*x

LESSON TWO

DEMONSTRATIVE ADJECTIVE

ce, cette, ces, cet = this, that, these, those
Like all adjectives, *ce* agrees in number and gender with the noun to
which it refers.

Masc.	ce	ce jardin – this, that garden
Fem.	cette	cette église – this, that church
Plural	ces	ces jardins – these, those gardens
		ces églises – these, those churches

Cet is used before a masculine singular noun beginning with a vowel or *h* mute. The *t* is sounded in liaison:

cet avion – this, that aeroplane
cet homme – this, that man

To make the distinction between 'this' and 'that', add *-ci* or *-là*:

par-ici – this way	par-là – that way
de ce côté-ci – on this side	de ce côté-là – on that side
cette fois-ci – this time	cette fois-là – that time
ces gens-ci – these people	ces gens-là – those people
ceci – this (pronoun)	cela, ça – that (pronoun)
voici – here is, here are	voilà – there is, there are, that's, those are

Ce is used impersonally in the forms *c'est* = that's, it's, and *ce sont* = those are, they're. It is used for identification, often combined with *cela, ça*:

Qu'est-ce que c'est? – What is it?
Qu'est-ce que c'est que ça? – What's that?
C'est une table – It's a table
C'est un Anglais – That's an Englishman
Ce sont des touristes – Those are tourists
Où ça? C'est par-là – Whereabouts is that? It's over there
Ça c'est un tableau – That's a picture
Ça c'est difficile – That's difficult

POSSESSIVE ADJECTIVE

(For possessive pronoun see p. 84)
The possessive adjective agrees in number and gender with the noun to which it refers, never with the person speaking:

Masc.	*Fem.*	*Plural*	
mon	ma	mes	my
ton	ta	tes	your (familiar)
son	sa	ses	his, her, its
notre	notre	nos	our
votre	votre	vos	your
leur	leur	leurs	their

The masculine forms *mon*, *ton*, *son* are used before a word beginning with a vowel or *h* mute, even if it is feminine.

Examples

1. Mes cheveux. 2. Ses tantes. 3. Leur travail. 4. Tes yeux. 5. Notre fille. 6. Mon idée (f). 7. Ton histoire (f). 8. Votre école (f). 9. Sa maison. 10. Son père et sa mère.

1. My hair. 2. His/her aunts. 3. Their work. 4. Your eyes. 5. Our daughter. 6. My idea. 7. Your story. 8. Your school. 9. His/her house. 10. His/her father and mother.

Exercise

Answer the following questions from the vocabulary given below. If you can't think of the noun, use *le truc* or *le machin*, both of which mean 'thing', 'whatsit, 'thingumajig'.

Qu'est-ce que c'est?   C'est . . . (mon oreille)
Qu'est-ce que c'est que ça?   Ça c'est . . . (votre doigt)
Où est . . . (ton bras)?   Voilà . . . (mon bras)

Le corps – the body

le cou – neck
la poitrine – chest
le coeur – heart
le sang – blood
une épaule – shoulder
le bras – arm
la main – hand
le doigt – finger
une ongle – nail
le dos – back
la jambe – leg
le genou – knee
le pied – foot

La tête – the head

les cheveux (m) – hair
le front – forehead
le visage – face
un oeil – eye
le sourcil – eyebrow
la paupière – eyelid
une oreille – ear
la bouche – mouth
la langue – tongue
la dent – tooth
le menton – chin
la peau – skin
la gorge – throat

Les vêtements (m) – clothes

le chapeau (-x) – hat(s)	le complet – suit
la chemise – shirt	le veston – jacket
la poche – pocket	le pardessus – overcoat
le pantalon – (pair of) trousers	un imperméable – raincoat
la chaussure – shoe	le manteau – woman's coat
la chaussette – sock	le bouton – button
la robe – dress	le mouchoir – handkerchief
la jupe – skirt	le gant – glove

ÊTRE	To be	NE PAS ÊTRE	Not to be
je suis	I am	je ne suis pas	I'm not
tu es	you are	tu n'es pas	you're not
il est	he/it is	il n'est pas	he/it isn't
elle est	she/it is	elle n'est pas	she/it isn't
nous sommes	we are	nous ne sommes pas	we aren't
vous êtes	you are	vous n'êtes pas	you aren't
ils sont	they are (m)	ils ne sont pas	they aren't
elles sont	they are (f)	elles ne sont pas	they aren't
suis-je?	am I?	ne suis-je pas?	aren't I? (am I not?)
es-tu?	are you?	n'es-tu pas?	aren't you?
est-il?	is he?	n'est-il pas?	isn't he?
sommes-nous?	are we?	ne sommes-nous pas?	aren't we?
êtes-vous?	are you?	n'êtes-vous pas?	aren't you?
sont-ils?	are they?	ne sont-ils pas?	aren't they?

Sentences

1. Qui êtes-vous? 2. Qui est-ce? 3. C'est un ami. 4. D'où es-tu? 5. Je suis de Londres. 6. Est-ce bien vrai? 7. Mais oui, bien sûr. 8. Ne sont-ils pas français? 9. Son copain est espagnol. 10. Ce n'est pas vrai!

1. Who are you? 2. Who is it? 3. It's a friend. 4. Where are you from? 5. I'm from London. 6. Is it really true? 7. Of course, certainly. 8. Aren't they French? 9. His mate's Spanish. 10. It isn't true!

C'est = it's, that's, in a non-specific sense.

Il est, elle est = it is, when referring to something which has been mentioned already. Often the subject of a sentence is put first and reinforced with the appropriate pronoun:

Et vos enfants, où sont-ils? – And where are your children?
Et Jean-Pierre, il n'est pas là? – And Jean-Pierre isn't there?
Ce journal, il est sur le tapis – This newspaper is on the carpet
Ma voiture, elle est au garage – My car is in the garage
Ces machins-là, ils sont dans l'armoire – Those things are in the wardrobe

QUESTIONS

You may ask a question by raising your voice at the end of the sentence:

Vous êtes anglais? Bien sûr, je suis anglais – Are you English? Certainly, I'm English
Il n'est pas français? Mais non, il est écossais – Isn't he French? No, no, he's Scottish

You may also ask a question by inversion of subject and verb:

Ce monsieur-là, est-il irlandais? – Is that gentleman Irish?
Ces gens-là, sont-ils gallois? – Are those people Welsh?

Strictly speaking, after interrogative words, inversion should be made:

Pardon Monsieur, la gare, s'il vous plaît, *où* est-elle? – Excuse me sir, *where* is the station, please?

Pourquoi ton vélo est-il toujours au garage? – *Why* is your bike always in the garage?

However, in speech, inversion is often ignored:

Qui c'est ce type-là? – *Who's* that bloke?
Le cinèma, *où* il est? – *Where's* the cinema?

THE NEGATIVE

Always write both parts of the negative: *ne . . . pas*. In speech, gloss over the *ne* and stress the *pas*:

je ne suis pas (ZHSWiPa)
ils ne sont pas (iSÔPa)
ce n'est pas vrai (SéPaVRé)

■ *Pronunciation*

i – t*i*roir, chem*i*se, su*i*s, qu*i*?, ou*i*
E – chauss*e*tte, v*ê*tements, t*ê*te
Wa – v*oi*ture, coul*oi*r, d*oi*gt, p*oi*trine, pourq*uoi*
OO – t*ou*jours, b*ou*ton, t*ou*riste

La maison – the house

les meubles (m) – furniture
la porte – door
un escalier – staircase
le tapis – carpet
le lit – bed
la chaise – chair
le fauteuil – armchair
la fenêtre – window
le cendrier – ashtray
le rideau (-x) – curtain
le tabouret – stool
une armoire – wardrobe
le placard – wall cupboard

les pièces (f) – rooms
la cuisine – kitchen
la chambre – bedroom
la salle à manger – dining-room
la salle de bains – bathroom
le salon – lounge, sitting room
les cabinets (m) – toilet
le jardin – garden
le bungalow – bungalow
le couloir – corridor
la terrasse – terrace
le balcon – balcony
la cave – cellar

Translation

Opposite the dining room, there is an armchair and a stool.
In the middle of the room, there's a staircase.
Outside the house, there's a garden and a terrace.
Watch out for the kids! There are cars in the street.
At the factory exit there's a bank and, next door, some garages.
There are some blokes in a car at the end of the road.

En face de la salle à manger, il y a un fauteuil et un tabouret.
Au milieu de la pièce, il y a un escalier.
Il y a un jardin et une terrasse à l'extérieur de la maison.
Attention aux gosses! Il y a des voitures dans la rue.
À la sortie de l'usine il y a une banque et, à côté, des garages.
Il y a des types dans une voiture au bout de la rue.

LESSON THREE

WORK

We have already met:

il est français – he is *a* Frenchman

In English we also say 'He is *a* doctor.' French leaves out the
article (*un*):

il est médicin – he is *a* doctor

Here is some useful work vocabulary:

le chômage – unemployment	le métier – career, job
le chômeur – unemployed man	la chômeuse – unemployed woman
un ouvrier – worker (male)	une ouvrière – worker (female)
un ingénieur – engineer	le mécanicien – mechanic
le technicien – technician	le pharmacien – chemist
le/la secrétaire – secretary	la sténo-dactylo – shorthand typist
le reporter – reporter	
le dentiste – dentist	le photographe – photographer

le professeur – teacher
le comptable – accountant
le(la)patron (-nne) – boss
le gendarme – traffic policeman
le flic – cop(per)
le manoeuvre – manual worker
le boulot – work (sl.)
la grève – strike
la grève de solidarité –
  sympathy strike
quel est votre métier? – what's
  your job?

une infirmière – nurse
le fonctionnaire – civil servant
le commis – clerk
une(e) employé(e) – employee
un agent – policeman
la police – police
le(la)retraité(e) – retired person
le job – holiday job
le/la gréviste – striker
les piquets de grève – strike
  pickets

STRESSED PRONOUNS

Je, tu, il, etc. are unstressed pronouns. Here are the forms of the stressed pronouns:

moi – I

nous – we

toi – you

vous – you

lui – he, it

eux – they (m)

elle – she, it

elles – they (f)

They are used:

(a) for emphasis, in addition to the unstressed pronoun:
    Moi, je suis commerçant, mais toi, tu es commis-voyageur
      – *I* am a businessman, but *you* are a commercial traveller
    Nous, nous sommes étudiants de Français; eux, ils sont
      professeurs – *We* are students of French; *they* are
      teachers
(b) when the pronoun stands alone:
    Qui est-ce? C'est lui – Who is it? It's him
(c) standing alone before *qui* = who:
    C'est vous qui êtes espagnol mais c'est lui qui est italien – It's
      you who are Spanish but it's *he* who's Italian
(d) with a double subject:
    Ce monsieur et moi, nous ne sommes pas français – This gentle-
      man and *I* are not French

(e) after prepositions:

devant moi – in front of me	derrière toi – behind you
entre nous – between us	sans lui – without him
selon eux – according to them (m)	vers elle – towards her
après toi – after you	sauf moi – except me
avec elles – with them (f)	malgré lui – in spite of him

Note: *chez* means at/to the house of, at/to someone's place:

chez moi – at my place

aller chez Simon – to go round to Simon's house

chez le médecin – at the doctor's

chez des amis – at the house of some friends

(f) with *à*, to indicate possession:

C'est à qui, ce tableau? C'est à moi – Whose picture is this?
  It's mine

C'est à qui ce machin? Eh attention, c'est à lui – Whose is this?
  Hey, look out, it's his

(g) *-même* – self, selves; *aussi* – too, also; *seul* – alone, are used to give further emphasis to the stressed pronoun.

Vous êtes facteur, n'est-ce pas? Je suis moi-même facteur –
  You're a postman, aren't you? I'm a postman myself

Alors, vous êtes américain? Lui aussi il est américain – You're
  American, then? He's American as well

Eux, ils sont étudiants? Non, lui seul est étudiant – Are they
  students? No, only he is a student

RELATIVE CLAUSES

Qui (who, which, that) is the subject of a relative clause:

La moto qui est devant la porte d'entrée est à moi – The motorbike (which is) in front of the door is mine

Voilà le monsieur qui est le responsable de l'usine – There's the
  gentleman (who is) in charge of the factory

In English, we often leave out the relative pronoun, but in French
you must put it in:

Voilà une histoire qui n'est pas drôle – That's not a funny story

Que (that) is a conjunction:

Tu es sûr que c'est une bibliothèque? Mais non, il est évident que c'est une librairie – Are you sure (that) it's a library? Of course not, it's obvious (that) it's a bookshop

AVOIR	To have	NE PAS AVOIR	Not to have
j'ai	I have	je n'ai pas	I haven't
tu as	you have	tu n'as pas	you haven't
il, elle a	he, she has	il, elle n'a pas	he, she hasn't
nous avons	we have	nous n'avons pas	we haven't
vous avez	you have	vous n'avez pas	you haven't
ils, elles ont	they have	ils, elles n'ont pas	they haven't

Interrogative: in the 3rd person singular, an extra *t* is added to help the sound flow: a-*t*-il? a-*t*-elle?

Il y a – there is, there are   Y a-t-il? – Is there, are there?
Il n'y a pas – there isn't, there   N'y a-t-il pas? – Isn't there?
  aren't   Aren't there?

■ Use of **avoir**

J'ai mal à la tête – I have a headache
Il n'a pas mal aux pieds? – Hasn't he got sore feet?
Avez-vous mal à la gorge? – Do you have a sore throat?
D'ici il y a une centaine de kilomètres à Dijon – From here it's about 100 km to Dijon
Combien de distance y a-t-il entre Bordeaux et Marseille? – How far is it from Bordeaux to Marseilles?
Combien y a-t-il d'ici à la gare? – How far is it from here to the station?
Y a-t-il plus de cinq minutes de marche? – Is it more than five minutes' walk?
Qu'est-ce qu'il y a? – What's the matter?
Il y a que je suis malade – I'm ill, that's what's wrong
Vous avez vos papiers, Monsieur? – Do you have your (identity) papers, sir?
Qu'est-ce qu'il a? – What's the matter with him?
Il a sûrement quelque chose – There's certainly something wrong with him

NUMBERS

zéro	0	cinq	5	dix	10	quinze	15
un, une	1	six	6	onze	11	seize	16
deux	2	sept	7	douze	12	dix-sept	17
trois	3	huit	8	treize	13	dix-huit	18
quatre	4	neuf	9	quatorze	14	dix-neuf	19

After 20, numbers become cumulative, adding digits to the base number:

20	vingt	21	vingt et un	22	vingt-deux
30	trente	31	trente et un	33	trente-trois
40	quarante	41	quarante et un	44	quarante-quatre
50	cinquante	51	cinquante et un	55	cinquante-cinq
60	soixante	61	soixante et un	66	soixante-six
70	soixante-dix	71	soixante et onze	77	soixante-dix-sept
80	quatre-vingts	81	quatre-vingt-un	88	quatre-vingt-huit
90	quatre-vingt-dix	91	quatre-vingt-onze	99	quatre-vingt-dix-neuf
100	cent	101	cent un	110	cent dix
200	deux cents	220	deux cent vingt	225	deux cent vingt-cinq
1,000	mille	1,120	mille cent vingt	20,000	vingt mille
10,000	un milliard	1,000,000	un million		

Combien (de)? = how much (of), how many (of)?
Cent and *quatre vingt* have no final *s* when followed by another digit:
trois cent dix-sept *but* deux cents hommes
Septante (70) and *nonante* (90) are dialect forms found in Belgium and Switzerland.

À peu près cent mètres – about 100 metres
Mille francs environ – about 1,000 francs

■ *Pronunciation*

Six and *dix* are pronounced (SiS) and (DiS) when counting and in liaison. Otherwise the final S sound is silent: dix francs (DiFRÃ).

But in *dix-sept*, *dix-huit* and *dix-neuf*, the liaison is made:
(DiSET), (DiSWiT), DiZNœF).

Vingt (VẼ), *vingt et un* (VẼTéœ̃), *cinq* (SẼK), *cinq cents* (SẼSÃ).

Practise the two nasal vowels (Ẽ) and (Ã) in *cinquante* (SẼKÃT)
and *cent vingt* (SÃVẼ).

Collectives

une dixaine de kilomètres – about 10 km
une douzaine de milles – a dozen miles
une vingtaine, une trentaine, etc. – about 20, 30, etc.
une centaine, des centaines – about 100, hundreds
des milliers de personnes – thousands of people
une quinzaine – a fortnight

Translate

13. 26. 66. 79. 80. 94. 111. 476. 999. 1,639. 5,937. 5,695,321.

AGE

In French you *have* an age:

Quel âge (m) avez-vous? – How old are you?
Elle a un an – She's one year old
J'ai quarante-cinq ans – I'm 45 years old
Il n'est pas vieux; il a vingt ans – He's not old; he's 20

Alternatively, use the phrase *être âgé(e)* – to be old:

Il est âgé de trente ans – He's 30 years old
Elle est âgée de onze ans – She's 11.

Note: un homme de quarante ans – a 40-year-old man
une femme d'un certain âge – a middle-aged woman

Exercise

1. Have you got a flat? 2. How many rooms are there where you
live? 3. How many bathrooms has your house got? 4. What's your
job? 5. My husband is a photographer but I'm an engineer. 6. My

wife and I are not French. 7. Whose is that thing there? 8. What's the matter? 9. Are you sure you're not ill? 10. He's 39 years old.

1. Avez-vous un appartement? 2. Combien de pièces y a-t-il chez vous (toi)? 3. Combien de salles de bains a votre (ta) maison? 4. Quel est votre (ton) métier? 5. Mon mari est photographe, mais moi, je suis ingénieur. 6. Ma femme et moi, nous ne sommes pas français. 7. C'est à qui ce machin-là? 8. Qu'est-ce qu'il y a? 9. Tu es sûr que tu n'es pas malade? 10. Il a trente-neuf ans.

LESSON FOUR

EN – preposition used without the definite article

Study its different meanings in the expressions given below:

un compte en banque – a bank account
en Angleterre, en France – in England, in France
en ville (f) – in the town
en province (m) – in the provinces (not in Paris)
en mer (f) – at sea (in a boat)
en tête de – at the head of
en queue (f) de – at the back of
en été (f) – in summer
en hiver (m) – in winter
en automne (m) – in autumn

en voyage (m) – travelling
en blue-jean – in jeans
en vacances (f pl) – on holiday
en crise – in a crisis
en colère – angry
en guerre – at war
en avril – in April
en réparation – under repair
en congé – on leave
en grève – on strike
en classe – in class
en prison – in prison
en cadeau – as a present

But: au printemps – in spring
à l'étranger (m) – abroad

à la campagne – in the country
au bord de la mer – at the seaside

Phrases

les arbres (m) sont en fleur (m) – the trees are in flower
le sucre en poudre (m), en morceaux (m pl) – granulated, lump sugar

un objet en bois (m) – a wooden object
une montre en or (m), en argent (m) – a gold, silver watch
un escalier en spirale (f) – a spiral staircase
aller en vélo (m), en voiture (f) ou en bateau (m) – to go by bicycle,
   car or boat
aller en car, en taxi (m), en moto – to go by coach, taxi, motorbike

But: aller par le train, à pied – to go by train, on foot

DEFINITE ARTICLE

The definite article is always required with nouns used in a general
or universal sense:

Le vin est bon mais le cognac est meilleur – Wine is good but brandy
   is better
Le travail est long mais la vie est courte – Work is long but life is
   short
Le bonheur est toujours en retard – Happiness is always late

Abstract nouns always need the definite article:

l'amour (m) – love   la mort – death
l'espoir (m) – hope   la colère – anger

Note that with *sans* the article is not needed:

sans doute (m) – without doubt
sans cesse (f) – ceaselessly

PARTITIVE ARTICLE

The addition of *de* to the definite article reduces the meaning of the
noun from the universal to the partial:

le vin – wine; du vin – some, any wine

le vin n'est pas cher – wine isn't expensive (wine in general)
vous avez du vin? – have you got any, some, wine? (partitive)

   In English we often omit the partitive article, but in French it
must always be expressed:

J'ai du lait, de la bière et de l'eau – I have milk, beer and water
Nous avons du beurre, du fromage et des oeufs – We have butter, cheese and eggs

DE alone

De without the definite article is used in two main cases:
(a) after a negative:
   Il n'y a pas *de* place (f) – There isn't any room
   Je n'ai pas *d*'argent – I haven't any money
   Il n'y a plus *de* trains – There are no more trains
   Tu n'as jamais *de* cigarettes – You've never got any cigarettes
(b) after expressions of quantity:

beaucoup de – a lot of, many	un manque de – a shortage of
assez de – enough	combien de? – how many? how much?
tellement de – so many	
un peu de – a little	trop de – too much, too many
moins de – less, fewer	peu de – few, little
un tas de – a load of, a great many of	tant de – so much, so many
	autant de – as much, as many
plus de – more	pas mal de – quite a lot

Sentences

1. Il y a beaucoup de chiens sur le trottoir. 2. Combien de gâteaux y a-t-il? 3. Nous n'avons jamais assez d'argent. 4. Vous avez trop de billets? 5. Un peu de silence, s'il vous plaît. 6. Peu d'ouvriers sont en chômage. 7. Aujourd'hui il y a moins de gens chez le dentiste. 8. Ce n'est pas vrai, tant d'Anglais en vacances! 9. J'ai un tas de problèmes. 10. Vous avez pas mal de bouteilles. 11. Il y a toujours un manque de travail.

1. There are a lot of dogs on the pavement. 2. How many cakes are there? 3. We never have enough money. 4. Have you got too many tickets? 5. A little silence, please. 6. Few workers are unemployed. 7. Today there are fewer people at the dentist. 8. I don't believe it (it's not true), so many English people on holiday! 9. I've got a load of problems. 10. You've got quite a lot of bottles. 11. There's always a shortage of work.

Content and composition

un kilo de fromage (m) – one kilo of cheese
cent grammes de pâté (m) – 100 grams of paté
un litre d'essence (f) – one litre of petrol
une dizaine de pommes (f) – about 10 apples
un morceau de pain (m) – a piece of bread
une boîte d'allumettes (f) – a box of matches
un verre de rouge (m) – a glass of red wine
une livre de jambon (m) – a pound of ham
une tasse de café (m) – a cup of coffee
un groupe de musiciens (m) – a group of musicians
une foule de spectateurs (m) – a crowd of spectators
une quantité de choses (f) – a quantity of things

Note however that the following expressions take *de* + definite article:

la plupart des enfants – *most of* the children
le reste du poulet – *the rest of* the chicken
encore de la bière, s'il vous plaît – *more* beer, please
à bien des égards (m) – in *many* respects

LE PRIX – PRICE

Price per quantity is expressed by the definite article:

Le beurre est trois francs les cent grammes – Butter is 3 francs per 100 grams
Il y a des pommes à dix francs la douzaine – There are apples at 10F per dozen
C'est quatre-vingts francs le kilo, Monsieur – It's 80F a kilo, sir

Note: Trois timbres à un franc vingt, s'il vous plaît, Madame – Three stamps at 1 franc 20 (centimes), please

Twenty years after the introduction of new francs, confusingly, most Frenchmen still count in old francs. One new franc = 100 old francs (anciens francs). Furthermore, in conversation, old or new francs are called *balles*:

new	*old*
cent francs =	dix mille (anciens) francs
cinquante balles =	cinq mille balles
vingt mille francs =	deux millions de francs

Exercise

Express the following in old and new francs:
10F, 1,000F, 500F, 150F, 200F, 20F, 10,000F.

Vocabulary – more avoir *phrases* (see also p. 24)

avoir raison – to be right	avoir besoin de – to need
avoir faim – to be hungry	avoir horreur de – to loathe
avoir froid – to be cold	avoir marre de – to be fed up with
avoir chaud – to be hot	avoir le droit de – to be allowed to
avoir sommeil – to be sleepy	avoir honte (de) – to be ashamed (of)
avoir tort – to be wrong	avoir peur (de) – to be afraid (of)
avoir soif – to be thirsty	avoir envie de – to want to

EN – PRONOUN

In expressions of quantity, *en* = of it, of them. There is no English equivalent; it would normally be understood.

Note the position of *en*, before the verb and, in negatives, after *ne*:

Combien en avez-vous? – How many (of them) have you got?
J'en ai seize – I've got 16 (of them)
Il y en a combien? – How much (of it) is there?
Il y en a cent grammes – There's 100 grams (of it)

Constructions with *de* also need *en* to complete the sense:

J'*en* ai besoin – I need it, them (I have need of it, them)
Vous n'*en* avez pas besoin – You don't need it (you don't have need of it)
Ils *en* ont horreur – They loathe it (they have horror of it)

J'*en* ai marre – I've had enough of it
Nous n'*en* avons pas peur – We're not afraid of it (haven't fear of it)

EN COURSE – SHOPPING (See also p. 117)

■ *Pronunciation*

oignon (WaNYŌ)   sandwich (SĀDWiTSH)
viande (VYĀD)   petit pain (PTiPĒ)
beurre (BœR)   saucisson (SOSiSŌ)
vingt-cinq (VĒSĒK)   cigarette (SiGaRET)

Vocabulary

désolé(e) – sorry   la pomme de terre – potato
qu'est-ce que – what (object)   le sandwich – sandwich
vous voulez – you want   le salami – salami
à votre service (m) – my   le paquet – packet
   pleasure (at your service)   la cigarette – cigarette
la viande – meat   les petits pains (m) – rolls
le jambon – ham   le tabac – tobacconist
le rôti – roast   la baguette – bread stick
le porc – pork   le pain aux raisins – Danish
le saucisson – sausage   pastry
la légume – vegetable   un oignon – onion
les petits pois (m) – peas   le fromage – cheese

■ *Conversation*

Bonjour Madame. Bonjour Monsieur. Vous désirez?
   Une tranche de pâte, s'il vous plaît. À peu près cent grammes.
Je suis désolée, Monsieur, mais nous n'en avons pas.
   Qu'est-ce que vous avez comme viande alors?
J'ai du jambon de Bayonne, du rôti de porc et du saucisson.
   Qu'est-ce que vous avez comme légumes?
Il y a des oignons, beaucoup de petits pois. Mais il n'y a pas de
pommes de terre.
   Vous avez des sandwichs?
Qu'est-ce que vous voulez comme sandwich? Nous en avons au

jambon, au salami, au fromage et au pâté.
  Une bouteille de vin, un paquet de cigarettes et une boîte d'allu-
  mettes, s'il vous plaît.
C'est a côté, les cigarettes, Monsieur, au tabac.
  Une baguette, une dizaine de petits pains et des pains aux raisins.
  J'en ai besoin de quatre.
Voilà, Monsieur.
  Allez, au revoir, Madame, et merci.
À votre service.

Good morning, madam. Good morning, sir. Can I help you?
  A slice of paté, please. About 100 grams.
I'm sorry, but we don't have any.
  What kind of meat have you got, then?
I've got Bayonne ham, roast pork and sausage.
  What kind of vegetables have you?
There are onions, lots of peas. But there aren't any potatoes.
  Have you got any sandwiches?
What kind of sandwiches do you want? We've got ham, salami,
cheese and paté.
  A bottle of wine, a packet of cigarettes and a box of matches,
  please.
Cigarettes are next door at the tobacconist's.
  A stick of bread, ten bread rolls and some Danish pastries. I need
  four.
Here you are, sir.
  Good-bye, then, and thank you.
My pleasure.

LESSON FIVE

REGULAR -ER VERBS

Present tense

These are the verbs whose infinitive ends in -er. They form the
largest group of regular verbs. Here is the model for conjugation:

donner	*to give*
je donne	I give, I am giving
tu donnes	you give, are giving
il donne	he gives, is giving
elle donne	she gives, is giving
nous donnons	we give, are giving
vous donnez	you give, are giving
ils donnent	they give, are giving
elles donnent	they give, are giving

Negative: il ne donne pas, vous ne donnez pas.
Interrogative: donne-t-il? donnez-vous?
Negative interrogative: ne donne-t-il pas? ne donnez-vous pas?

Imperative – commands

-er verbs drop the *s* in the second person singular:

2nd sing.	donne – give	ne donne pas – don't give
1st plural	donnons – let's give	ne donnons pas – don't let's give, let's not give
2nd plural	donnez – give	ne donnez pas – don't give

Irregular imperatives:

être (to be): sois, soyons, soyez
avoir (to have): aie, ayons, ayez
savoir (to know): sache, sachons, sachez

Some regular -er verbs:

aimer – to like, love	hésiter – to hesitate
arriver – to arrive, happen	informer – to tell
chanter – to sing	inviter – to invite
chercher – to look for	monter – to go up
décider – to decide	parler – to speak, talk
demander – to ask	porter – to carry, wear
écouter – to listen to	poser – to put
empêcher – to prevent	quitter – to leave
entrer – to go in	regretter – to be sorry
s'excuser – to excuse oneself	rester – to stay
fermer – to shut	travailler – to work
fumer – to smoke	trouver – to find

Exercise

1. We don't work. 2. He loves. 3. You (sing.) do not listen. 4. Ask!
(sing.) 5. Come in! (pl). 6. Let's be. 7. They (f) are leaving. 8. She is
going up. 9. Listen! (pl). 10. I find. 11. We decide. 12. He is sorry.
13. Sing! (pl). 14. I am speaking. 15. He is wearing.

1. Nous ne travaillons pas. 2. Il aime. 3. Tu n'écoutes pas. 4.
Demande! 5. Entrez! 6. Soyons. 7. Elles quittent. 8. Elle monte. 9.
Écoutez! 10. Je trouve. 11. Nous décidons. 12. Il regrette. 13.
Chantez! 14. Je parle. 15. Il porte.

Verb usage

Continuer *à* poser des questions *à* quelqu'un – To keep on asking
  someone questions
Demander *à* mon voisin *de* parler plus haut – To ask my neighbour
  to speak louder
Inviter quelqu'un à chanter une chanson – To ask someone to sing a
  song
Aller chercher le médecin – To go and get the doctor
Il ne cherche pas *à* s'excuser – He isn't trying to excuse himself
Il décide *de* renoncer *à* fumer – He decides to give up smoking
Je regrette *de* vous informer que . . . – I regret to tell you that . . .
Montez vos bagages *dans* le car, Monsieur – Put your luggage into
  the bus, sir
Il hésite *à* entrer *dans* le musée – He hesitates to go into the
  museum
Donner le feu vert *à* quelqu'un – To give someone the go-ahead
Parlez plus bas, s'il vous plaît – Speak more quietly, please

MORE INTERROGATIVES

Est-ce que? before a statement turns it into a question and avoids
inversion:

Est-ce qu'il y a des Allemands dans le car? – Are there any
  Germans in the coach?
Est-ce que vous êtes sûr? Est-ce que tu es certain? – Are you sure?
  Are you certain?

N'est-ce pas = isn't it? aren't there? etc.

Cette idée, elle est drôle, n'est-ce pas? – It's a funny idea, isn't it?
Il y a des trains tout le temps, n'est-ce pas? – There are always
    trains, aren't there?

Qu'est-ce que . . .

We have met *qu'est-ce que c'est?*, meaning, literally, 'what is it that
it is?'

   Qu'est-ce que is also used to express surprise – what a . . .!
How . . . it is!

Qu'est-ce qu'il est joli, ce pantalon!
Ce monsieur, qu'est-ce qu'il est amusant!
Qu'est-ce que vous êtes bête!

What a pretty pair of trousers!
What an amusing man that is!
How silly you are!

ON – indefinite pronoun

On is the most widely used pronoun. It can mean: I, we, you, one,
someone, or it can replace the passive voice (see lesson fifteen). The
following verb is always in the 3rd person singular:

On est bien ici – We're OK here
On reste ou on ne reste pas? – Are we staying or not?
Attention, on a besoin de vous – Look out, they need you (you are
    wanted)
Ici on parle anglais – Here we speak English

   A characteristic way of saying 'We do something' is *Nous, on* . . .

Nous, on va en vacances – We're going on holiday
Nous, on y va par le train – We're going by train

LES JOURS DE LA SEMAINE – THE DAYS OF THE WEEK

These are all masculine and have no initial capitals.

lundi – Monday

mardi – Tuesday

mercredi – Wednesday

jeudi – Thursday

vendredi – Friday

samedi – Saturday

dimanche – Sunday

huit jours – a week

quinze jours – a fortnight

aujourd'hui – today

demain – tomorrow

hier – yesterday

avant-hier – day before yesterday

après-demain – day after tomorrow

la semaine – the week

le jour – day

le weekend – at the weekend

le lundi – on Mondays

le lendemain – the next day

un après-midi – an afternoon

dernier – last

prochain – next

Jeudi soir, vendredi matin, samedi prochain, mardi dernier – Thursday evening, Friday morning, next Saturday, last Tuesday

C'est (on est) (nous sommes) aujourd'hui dimanche – Today is Sunday

Le mercredi, je suis toujours chez moi – I'm always at home on Wednesdays

Note the difference between a fixed time and the duration of time:

un jour (m) – one day

demain soir (m) – tomorrow evening

ce matin (m) – this morning

l'an prochain – next year

pendant la journée (f) – during the day

une soirée (f) agréable – a pleasant evening

passer la matinée (f) – to spend the morning

en cours d'année (f) – in the course of the year

EXPRESSIONS OF TIME

une heure de route – an hour's drive

un ouvrier payé à l'heure – a worker paid by the hour

la semaine de quarante heures – forty-hour week

la journée de huit heures – eight-hour day
de jour en jour – from day to day
au jour le jour – day by day
de temps en temps – from time to time
être en retard – to be late
être de bonne heure – to be early
il y a un mois – one month ago
tôt ou tard – sooner or later
bien tard – very late
trop tard – too late
plusieurs fois par jour – several times a day
au bout de quelques instants – after a few moments

■ *Pronunciation*

avant-hier (aVĀTYER)
bagages (BaGAZH)
n'est-ce pas? (NESPa?)
aujourd'hui (OZHOORDwi)
PCV (PéSéVé)

renseignements (RĀSENYeMĀ)
plusieurs (PLUZYœR)
information (ĒFoRMaSYŌ)
samedi (SaMDi)
numéro (NUMéRO)

LE TÉLÉPHONE – THE TELEPHONE

Digits in telephone numbers are spoken as follows:
22 – 35 – 14 – le vingt-deux, trente-cinq, quatorze
01 – 28 – 92 – le zero un, vingt-huit, quatre-vingt-douze

Vocabulary

je voudrais – I should like
raccrocher – to hang up
exister – to exist
consulter – to consult
composer – to dial
essayer – to try
téléphoner – to telephone
laisser – to leave
occupé – engaged
le demandeur – caller
un abonné – subscriber
le numéro – number

un annuaire – telephone directory
un indicatif – code number
les renseignements (m) – information
de nouveau – again
une attente – wait, delay
en PCV – reversed charges
un message – message
être là – to be in
il n'est pas là – he's not here

■ *Conversation*

Allo! Mademoiselle, je voudrais le 42–64–73–76 à Paris, s'il vous plaît.

Un instant, Monsieur, ne raccrochez pas . . .

Allo! C'est le 42–64–73–76?

Le numéro que vous demandez n'existe pas. Consultez l'annuaire.

Quel numéro désirez-vous? Mais pour Paris c'est automatique. Composez le numéro vous-même. L'indicatif de Paris c'est le 16 et le 1.

. . . 'Il n'y a plus d'abonné au numéro que vous demandez. Consultez le service de renseignements.'

Votre numéro est occupé, Monsieur. Essayez de nouveau dans vingt minutes.

Allo, renseignements, je vous écoute.

Je voudrais téléphoner à Paris avec ma carte. Où puis-je utiliser ma carte?

Il y a sûrement une autre cabine à côté qui accepte les cartes.

Merci beaucoup.

Allo! Monsieur Leclerc?

Je suis désolée mais il n'est pas là. Vous voulez laisser un message?

Hello! I should like Paris 42–64–73–76 please, miss.

One moment, sir. Don't hang up.

Hello! Is that 42–64–73–76?

The number you're asking for does not exist. Consult the directory.

Which number do you want? But it's automatic to Paris. Dial the number yourself. The code for Paris is 16 and 1.

. . . 'There is no longer a subscriber at the number you are dialling. Consult the Information Service.'

Your number is engaged. Try again in 20 minutes.

Hello, information service (I am listening).

I should like to make a call to Paris with my card. Where can I use my card?

There is sure to be another booth next to you which takes cards.

Thank you very much.

Hello, Monsieur Leclerc?

I'm sorry, but he isn't here. Do you want to leave a message?

LESSON SIX

IRREGULAR VERBS

Present tense

	aller – to go	*venir – to come*
je	vais	viens
tu	vas	viens
il, elle	va	vient
nous	allons	venons
vous	allez	venez
ils, elles	vont	viennent
past participle:	allé	venu

	faire – to do, make	*prendre – to take*
je	fais	prends
tu	fais	prends
il, elle	fait	prend
nous	faisons	prenons
vous	faites	prenez
ils, elles	font	prennent
past participle:	fait	pris

The interrogative form of *aller* needs an extra *t* in the 3rd person sing.: Va-t-il? Va-t-elle?

Imperative

va – allons – allez
viens – venons – venez
fais – faisons – faites
prends – prenons – prenez

Note: Vas-y! Allons-y! Allez-y, les gars! – Go on! Let's go! Go on, lads!

Exercise

1. We make. 2. They (f) are taking. 3. Let's go! 4. He's coming.

5. Are you (pl) going? 6. Come (sing.) here! 7. I am doing. 8. Are we taking? 9. I'm not going. 10. Aren't you (pl) coming?

1. Nous faisons. 2. Elles prennent. 3. Allons-y! 4. Il vient. 5. Allez-vous? 6. Viens ici! 7. Je fais. 8. Prenons-nous? 9. Je ne vais pas. 10. Ne venez-vous pas?

Verb usage

Combien ça fait? – How much is that?
Ça fait cent francs – That's 100F
Cela ne fait pas assez – That isn't enough
Ça ne fait rien – It doesn't matter
Je n'ai rien à faire avec lui – I've got nothing to do with him

IMMEDIATE FUTURE – ALLER + INFINITIVE

Tu *vas venir* ou tu *vas rester* là? – Are you going to come or stay there?
Vous *allez fusiller* le patron? – Are you going to shoot the boss?
On *va acheter* des souvenirs (m)? – Are we going to buy souvenirs?
Elle *va passer* la soirée chez nous – She's going to spend the evening with us
On *va être* en retard – We're going to be late

IMMEDIATE PAST – VENIR DE + INFINITIVE

Je viens *de traverser* la Manche – I've just crossed the Channel
Il vient *d'enfermer* le dentiste dans son bureau – He has just locked the dentist in his office
Nous venons *de passer* deux jours à la campagne – We've just spent two days in the country
Je viens *d'arriver* et je vais rester – I've just arrived and I'm going to stay

■ LA SANTÉ – HEALTH

Aller is also used to describe your health:

Comment allez-vous? Comment vas-tu? – How are you?
Je vais très bien – I'm fine

Je vais mieux – I'm better
Je vais de mieux en mieux – I'm better and better
Ça va? Comment ça va? – How are you?
Oui, ça va bien – I'm OK

But note also:

Je suis en pleine forme – I'm in top form
Aujourd'hui je suis un peu malade – I'm not very well today
Je suis enrhumé – I've got a cold
Je viens d'attraper un rhume – I've just caught a cold

INTERROGATIVE ADJECTIVES

	Sing.	Plural	
Masc.	quel	quels	what, what kind of,
Fem.	quelle	quelles	which?

Quel is used in direct questions:

De quelle couleur sont ses cheveux? – What colour is his, her hair?
Quelle est votre adresse? – What is your address?
Quel est votre nom? – What is your name?
Quel est votre métier? – What is your job?
Vous êtes de quelle nationalité? – What nationality are you?
Quels sont ces messieurs? – Who are these gentlemen?
Quel est votre avis? – What's your opinion?

Quel is also used in exclamations to mean 'What a . . . !'

Quel magnifique coup de pied! – What a magnificent kick!
Quelle surprise! quel idiot! – What a surprise! what an idiot!

Exercise

1. Which man? 2. What cheese? 3. What an evening! 4. Which roads? 5. Which hotels?

1. Quel homme? 2. Quel fromage? 3. Quelle soirée! 4. Quelles rues? 5. Quels hôtels?

■ L'HEURE – TELLING THE TIME

Quelle heure est-il? – What time is it?

Pardon, Monsieur, vous avez l'heure? – Excuse me, sir, can you tell me the time?

Il est une heure, deux heures, etc. – It's 1 o'clock, 2 o'clock, etc.

midi, minuit (both m) – noon, midnight

huit heures et quart – a quarter past 8

six heures moins le (un) quart – a quarter to 6

midi (minuit) et demi – half past twelve

trois heures et demie – half past three

onze heures trente, une heure dix – 11.30, ten past one

deux heures moins vingt – twenty to two (lit. less twenty)

It is more usual to refer to the 24-hour clock:

dix-huit heures quarante-cinq – 6.45 pm

vingt et une heures trente – 9.30 pm

dix-neuf heures zéro six – 7.06 pm

Alternatively:

à onze heures du matin – at 11 in the morning

à dix heures et demie du soir – at 10.30 in the evening

à deux heures de l'après-midi – at 2 in the afternoon

à cinq heures juste(s) – at exactly 5

une demi-heure, un quart d'heure – half an hour, a quarter of an hour

trois bons quarts d'heure – a good three-quarters of an hour

les magasins sont ouverts de huit heures à midi – the shops are open from 8 to 12

une pharmacie ouverte à toute heure – a 24-hour chemist

Exercise

Express the following in two different ways:

3.44; 17.40; 24.30; 11.17; 21.02; 1.25; 14.35; 12.05; 16.45

Y – THERE

Y usually means 'there', and stands immediately before the verb:

Vous y allez? Oui, j'y vais – Are you going (there)? Yes, I'm going (there).

Nous y allons tout de suite – We're going (there) straight away

On y va ou on n'y vas pas? – Are we going (there) or not?

Pensez-y! – Think about it! (on it)

Ça y est is a useful phrase meaning 'That's it', 'There we are', 'That's OK'.

Vous en avez assez, Monsieur? – Have you got enough, sir?

Oui, oui, ça y est – Yes, yes, that's fine

NEGATIVES

ne . . . rien – nothing

ne . . . personne – nobody

ne . . . jamais – never

ne . . . plus – no more

ne . . . que – only

ni . . . ni . . . ne – neither . . . nor

nul(le) . . . ne – no (adj.)

Il n'y a rien d'intéressant – There's nothing interesting there

Vous n'allez rien dire? – Aren't you going to say anything?

Rien n'est ouvert – Nothing is open

Qu'est-ce qu'il y a? Rien – What's wrong? Nothing

Il n'y a rien à faire – There's nothing to do, to be done

Il n'y a personne – There's nobody there

Je ne vais déranger personne – I'm not going to upset anybody

Personne ne va venir – No one's going to come

Qui c'est? Personne – Who is it? Nobody

Je n'ai jamais de chance – I never have any luck

Vous n'y allez jamais? – You never go there?

Jamais vous n'êtes chez vous – You're never at home

Fais attention, si jamais tu vas à Paris – Look out if ever you go to Paris

Il n'y a plus d'espoir – There's no more hope

Je n'y vais plus – I'm not going there any more

Je ne vais plus jamais y aller – I'm not going there ever again

Je n'ai que cent balles sur moi – I've only got a franc on me

Je n'ai plus rien – I've nothing left

Ce ne sont que des touristes – They are only tourists

Il n'y a ni beurre, ni potage – There's neither butter nor soup

Ni elle, ni moi n'est content – Neither she nor I is happy
Tu ne vas être heureux nulle part – Nowhere will you be happy

COMMENT DEMANDER SON CHEMIN – HOW TO ASK THE WAY

Vocabulary

le chemin – way	surtout – especially
une exposition – exhibition	même – same
le boulevard – street	presque – almost
le trottoir – pavement	tout près – quite close
le Palais – palace	vous vous trompez – you are
la justice – justice	mistaken
la cathédrale – cathedral	vous sortez – you go out
le feu rouge – traffic lights	descendez – go down
une université – university	tournez – turn
le passant – passer-by	tomber – to fall
difficile – difficult	marcher – to walk
facile – easy	voir – to see
deuxième – second	remonter – to go up

■ *Pronunciation*

e – le, faisons, peu, descendez, chemin, prenez
E – presque, faites, prennent, deuxième, même

■ *Conversation*

Pardon, Madame, quel est le chemin de l'exposition, s'il vous plaît?
Est-ce que le chemin est difficile à trouver?
   O, mais c'est facile. Ce n'est pas très loin. Vous sortez d'ici, à
gauche; allez tout droit jusqu'au boulevard Saint-Michel. Descendez le boulevard, tournez à droite, prenez la deuxième rue à
gauche, et vous aller tomber dans la rue des Écoles. Vous continuez
de marcher sur le même trottoir. Si vous regardez à votre gauche,
vous allez voir le Palais de Justice et la cathédrale de Notre Dame.
Vous passez un feu rouge; prenez la rue à droite, remontez la rue de
l'Université, et vous y êtes!

Merci beaucoup.

Il n'y a pas de quoi. Il est presque impossible de perdre son chemin. Mais si jamais vous vous trompez de chemin, demandez à un passant. C'est tout près de la Gare Saint-Lazare. Mais surtout, ne passez pas la Seine! Allez, au revoir et bonne chance!

(Une heure plus tard)

Pour aller à l'exposition, s'il vous plaît?

Vous y allez à pied? Mais c'est bien loin d'ici. Prenez le métro.

Excuse me, madam, which is the way to the exhibition, please? Is the way difficult to find?

Oh, but it's easy! It isn't far. You go out of here, to the left, go straight on until the boulevard Saint-Michel. Go down the street, turn to the right, take the second road on the left and you will be in (fall into) Schools Street. Keep on walking on the same pavement. If you look to the left you will see the Palace of Justice and the Cathedral of Notre Dame. You go past some traffic lights, take the road on the right, go up University Street and you're there!

Thank you very much.

Don't mention it. It's almost impossible to lose your way. But if ever you lose the way, ask a passer-by. It's quite close to Saint-Lazare station. But above all, don't cross the Seine! Good-bye and good luck!

(One hour later)

The way to the Exhibition, please?

Are you going on foot? But it's a long way from here. Take the underground.

LESSON SEVEN

IRREGULAR VERBS

Present tense

	dire – to say	*voir – to see*	*mettre – to put*	*connaître – to know*
je	dis	vois	mets	connais
tu	dis	vois	mets	connais
il	dit	voit	met	connaît

nous	disons	voyons	mettons	connaissons
vous	dites	voyez	mettez	connaissez
ils	disent	voient	mettent	connaissent
past p.:	dit	vu	mis	connu

Conjugated like *prendre* are:

apprendre – to learn
comprendre – to understand

surprendre – to surprise
reprendre – to take again

Conjugated like *mettre* are:

Conjugated like *voir* is:

omettre – to omit
permettre – to permit, allow

prévoir – to foresee

Exercise

1. Doesn't he know? 2. Do you (sing.) see? 3. We are putting. 4. He says. 5. They foresee. 6. We are not learning. 7. Allow! (pl). 8. Let's put.

1. Ne connaît-il pas? 2. Vois-tu? 3. Nous mettons. 4. Il dit. 5. Ils prévoient. 6. Nous n'apprenons pas. 7. Permettez! 8. Mettons.

Verb usage

A verb following direct speech is inverted:
'Comment ça va?' *dit-il.* – 'How are you?' he says.

Il dit qu'il a besoin d'argent – He says he needs money
Dire quelque chose à voix basse – To say something quietly (in a low voice)
C'est plus facile à dire qu'à faire – It's easier said than done
Ne pas voir plus loin que le bout de son nez – Not to see farther than the end of one's nose
Je vais apprendre à parler français – I'm going to learn French
Apprendre à quelqu'un à faire quelque chose – To teach someone to do something
Je n'y comprends rien – I don't understand it at all
Son patron va permettre à Serge de ne pas venir travailler demain – His boss will allow Serge not to come to work tomorrow
Je passe devant vous. Vous permettez? – I'm going in front of you. Do you mind?

INTERROGATIVE PRONOUNS

Who?	*Subject*	Qui? Qui est-ce qui? (KiESKi?)
	Object	Qui? Qui est-ce que (KiESKe?)
	With preposition	Qui?
What?	*Subject*	Qu'est-ce qui? (KESKi?)
	Object	Que? Qu'est-ce que? (KESKe?)
	With preposition	Quoi?

Qui est là? Qui êtes-vous? – Who's there? Who are you?
Qui est-ce qui chante? – Who is singing?
Qui est-ce que vous cachez? – Who are you hiding?
Qu'est-ce que vous cachez? – What are you hiding?
Avec qui allez-vous? – Who are you going with?
Qu'est-ce qui arrive? – What's happening?
Qu'y a-t-il? – What's the matter?
Que faire? – What should we do?
Il n'y a pas de quoi – Not at all
Quoi de neuf? Quoi – What's new? what?
À quoi jouez-vous? – What are you playing at?

Do you remember the first chapter?

Qu'est-ce que c'est que ça?
Qu'est-ce que c'est que ce truc-là?

Other interrogatives and replies

Comment il est, votre appartement? – What's your flat like?
Quand venez-vous? – When are you coming?
À quelle heure va-t-il arriver? – What time is he going to come?
Pourquoi vont-ils venir? – Why are they going to come?
Parce qu'ils sont en vacances – Because they are on holiday

Exercise

1. How much is that? 2. Who are you looking for? 3. Where shall I put the car? 4. What are we going to do? 5. What have you (pl) just said? 6. When are you (sing.) going to learn something? 7. Whom do you (pl) know in Paris? 8. Why is he never at home? 9. Because he works an 8-hour day at the office. 10. Who are you (pl) playing with?

1. Combien ça fait? 2. Qui cherchez-vous? 3. Où est-ce que je vais mettre la voiture? 4. Qu'est-ce que nous allons faire? 5. Qu'est-ce que vous venez de dire? 6. Quand vas-tu apprendre quelque chose? 7. Qui connaissez-vous à Paris? 8. Pourquoi n'est-il jamais chez lui? 9. Parce qu'il travaille huit heures par jour au bureau. 10. Avec qui jouez-vous?

AGREEMENT OF ADJECTIVES

Feminine

An adjective agrees in number and gender with the noun to which it refers. The feminine is regularly formed by adding *e* to the masculine. However, the commonest adjectives are often irregular.

Regular

vert(e) – green	joli(e) – pretty
noir(e) – black	mauvais(e) – bad
bleu(e) – blue	lourd(e) – heavy
petit(e) – small	vilain(e) – ugly
grand(e) – big, great	court(e) – short
haut(e) – high, loud	

Irregular

x to *se*	*x* or *s* to *sse*
heureux(se) – happy	bas(sse) – low
jaloux(se) – jealous	gras(sse) – fatty, oily
spacieux(se) – spacious	las(sse) – tired
	gros(sse) – big, fat
	faux(sse) – false
	roux(sse) – reddish
	épais(sse) – thick
	exprès(esse) – express

No change	*et* to *ète*
rouge – red	*complet*(ète) – full
jaune – yellow	inquiet(ète) – worried
jeune – young	secret(ète) – secret
large – wide	

er to *ère*
cher(ère) – dear, expensive
leger(ère) – light
premier(ère) – first
dernier(ère) – last

Feminine in (lle)
gentil(lle) – nice, kind
pareil(lle) – same, similar
actuel(lle) – present (time)
cruel(lle) – cruel
nul(lle) – no, not a
beau(belle) – fine, beautiful
nouveau(elle) – new (different)
vieux(vieille) – old
fou (folle) – mad, crazy

Double the consonant
bon(nne) – good
ancien(nne) – old, former
net(tte) -- clean
sot(tte) – silly

Others
blanc(che) – white
franc(che) – frank
sec(èche) – dry
doux(ce) – soft, sweet
long(gue) – long
vif(ve) – lively
neuf(ve) – (brand) new

These adjectives are so common that the feminine forms will soon become familiar.

But note that five common adjectives and *ce* have a special form used before masculine nouns beginning with a vowel or *h* mute:

beau (belle) – bel
nouveau (nouvelle) – nouvel
vieux (vieille) – vieil

fou (folle) – fol
mou (molle) – mol
ce (cette) – cet

un bel appartement – a fine flat
le Nouvel An – the New Year
un vieil homme – an old man
un fol anglais – a mad Englishman
un mol édredon – a soft eiderdown
cet an – this year

Plural

These are much easier. The plural is regularly formed by adding *s* to the singular. Since all feminine singular adjectives end in *e*, all feminine plurals end in *es* – rouges, bonnes, vieilles, etc.

The masculine plural is usually formed by adding *s* to the masculine singular – verts, bleus, longs, etc.

But notice that those ending in *s* or *x* do not change – doux, douce, *doux*, douces; gros, grosse, *gros*, grosses.

Those ending in *eau* add *x* – beau, belle, *beaux*, belles; nouveau, nouvelle, *nouveaux*, nouvelles.

Most ending in *al* become *aux*, but many merely add *s* – communal, *communaux* (communal); final, *finals* (final).

Position

Adjectives usually follow the noun, particularly when they are long or unwieldy. Two adjectives referring to the same noun are linked by *et*:

un coup de chance extraordinaire – an amazing stroke of luck
des voitures françaises – French cars
une vache blanche et noire – a black and white cow

Short adjectives and those you want to emphasise usually precede the noun:

un joli chapeau rond – a pretty, round hat
une jolie petite maison – a pretty little house
un fantastique coup de pied – a fantastic kick

A few adjectives change their meaning according to their position.

un ancien élève – a former pupil; une ville ancienne – an ancient town
un homme pauvre – a poor (not rich) man; un pauvre homme – an unfortunate man
un cher ami – a dear friend; une robe chère – an expensive dress
un homme grand – a tall man; un grand homme – a great man
ma propre maison – my own house; les mains propres – clean hands

Agreement is still made when the adjective stands alone:

Les Français sont sympas – The French are really nice
Je suis inquiète – I (f) am worried
une fille, jolie comme une fleur – a girl, pretty as a flower

An adjective describing nouns of both genders takes the masculine form:

les hommes and les femmes anglais – English men and women

Exercise

1. In a low voice. 2. In a loud voice. 3. Red hair. 4. At the present time. 5. Peas. 6. Last year. 7. Wide roads. 8. An old factory.

1. À voix basse. 2. À haute voix. 3. Les cheveux roux. 4. À l'heure actuelle. 5. Les petits pois. 6. L'an dernier. 7. Des rues larges (spacieuses). 8. Une vieille usine.

VOUS AVEZ QUELQUE CHOSE À DÉCLARER? – ANYTHING TO DECLARE?

Vocabulary

la douane – customs
la frontière – border
la fiche – form
le nom – surname
le prénom – forename
le passeport – passport
le lieu – place
le départ – departure
la destination – destination
le douanier – customs officer
la fois – time (occasion)
les pièces d'identité – identity papers

avant de – before (+ inf.)
chaque – each
là-dessous – under it
être obligé de – to have to
remplir – to fill
examiner – to inspect
on doit – you must
visiter – visit
une valise – suitcase
le parfum – perfume
l'alcool (m) – alcohol
la contrebande – smuggling
le contrôle – control

■ *Conversation*

Avant de passer une frontière, on est souvent obligé de remplir une fiche de police. On met son nom et son prénom, le numéro du passeport et le lieu de son départ et de sa destination. Les douaniers ont le droit d'examiner les bagages. Chaque fois qu'on passe le contrôle, on doit montrer ses pièces d'identité.

Votre passeport, s'il vous plaît? Combien de temps allez-vous rester en France? Quels bagages avez-vous?

Voici mon passeport. Je n'ai qu'une petite valise et les deux gros paquets là-bas. Je n'ai rien à déclarer.

Vous n'avez pas de cigarettes, d'alcool, de parfum? Pourquoi pas? Il est lourd, votre pardessus. Combien de bouteilles de vin cachez-vous là-dessous? Et vos paquets, eux aussi sont assez lourds.

Je ne fais pas la contrebande, Monsieur. C'est la première fois que je visite la France.

La première fois? Allez, passez, Monsieur. Le bureau de change est à votre gauche. Voilà votre passeport. La première visite en France? Profitez-en, Monsieur!

Before crossing a border, you often have to fill in a police form. You put your surname and first name, the passport number and the place of your departure and destination. The customs officials may examine your luggage. Each time you pass the control, you have to show your identity papers.

Your passport, please? How long will you stay in France? What luggage have you got?

Here's my passport. I've only got a little case and the two big parcels over there. I have nothing to declare.

You don't have any cigarettes, alcohol, perfume? Why not? Your overcoat is heavy. How many bottles of wine are you hiding under it? And those parcels of yours, they're pretty heavy too.

I am not a smuggler. It's the first time that I've visited France.

The first time? Go on, go through, sir. The exchange office is on your left. There's your passport. Your first visit to France? Enjoy it, sir!

LESSON EIGHT

REFLEXIVE VERBS

These are verbs which appear in the dictionary with *se* in front of them:

se lever, se laver, se comporter – to get up, to wash, to behave

Most verbs involve doing something to someone or something else, but reflexive verbs involve doing something to yourself:

je me lave = I'm washing myself = I wash

Here the action of the rebounds on the doer – 'I' is the person who both washes and is washed. Some verbs are always reflexive, most can be made reflexive. They are conjugated like ordinary verbs with the addition of the reflexive pronoun – *me, te, se, nous, se.*

Present tense

se laver – to wash
je me lave
tu te laves
il se lave
nous nous lavons
vous vous lavez
ils se lavent

ne pas se laver – not to wash
je ne me lave pas
tu ne te laves pas
il ne se lave pas
nous ne nous lavons pas
vous ne vous lavez pas
ils ne se lavent pas

Imperative

lave-toi! ne te lave pas!
lavons-nous! ne nous lavons pas!
lavez-vous! ne vous lavez pas!

s'en aller – to go away
je m'en vais, tu t'en vas, nous nous en allons, etc.
il ne s'en va pas, vous ne vous en allez pas, etc.
Imperative: va-t-en, allons-nous-en, allez-vous-en

Verb usage

Comment se comporte-t-il? – How is he behaving?
Tu te comportes comme un idiot – You're behaving like an idiot
Il s'arrête – He stops (himself)
Arrêtez la voiture – Stop the car
Je vais habiller mon fils en militaire – I'm going to dress my son as a soldier
Le policier s'habille en civil – The policeman is dressed in plain clothes
Tu vas ennuyer tes parents – You're going to bore your parents
Vous vous ennuyez chez ma tante? – Are you bored at my aunt's?

Tu inquiètes toujours tes copains – You always worry your friends
Il s'inquiète de vous – He's worried about you

Reflexive verbs can also be used to mean that people are doing things to each other:

Nous nous envoyons des lettres (f) – We're sending each other
  letters
Ils se serrent la main – They are shaking hands (with each other)

Some reflexive verbs

se demander – to wonder
se méfier de – to mistrust
se renseigner – to make
  enquiries
se moquer de – to make fun of
s'éloigner de – to move away
  from

se coucher – to go to bed
se développer – to develop
s'intéresser à – to be
  interested in
se tromper (de) – to make a
  mistake (about)
s'appeler – to be called

Comment vous appelez-vous? Je m'appelle Henri (see p. 70) – What's your name? I'm called Henry

REGULAR -IR AND -RE VERBS

Present tense

These are the other two large groups of regular verbs:

	finir – to finish	*vendre – to sell*
je	finis	vends
tu	finis	vends
il	finit	vend
nous	finissons	vendons
vous	finissez	vendez
ils	finissent	vendent
past p.:	fini	vendu

Imperative

finis, finissons, finissez   vends, vendons, vendez

Conjugated like these models are:

agir – to act	attendre – to wait for
choisir – to choose	défendre – to forbid
réfléchir – to think, ponder	descendre – to go down, get down
ralentir – to slow down	entendre – to hear, understand
remplir – to fill	s'étendre – to stretch, extend
réussir à – to succeed in	interrompre – to interrupt
saisir – to seize, grab	perdre – to lose
surgir – to surge, loom up	se produire – to take place
	répondre – to answer

Exercise

1. We're interested in the cinema. 2. You're (pl) on the wrong road. 3. Are you (sing.) going to bed? 4. Move (pl) away! 5. I'm thinking. 6. We don't understand. 7. We've just lost. 8. Let's choose. 9. Slow (pl) down! 10. Don't worry (sing.)!

1. Nous nous intéressons au cinéma. 2. Vous vous trompez de chemin. 3. Te couches-tu? 4. Éloignez-vous! 5. Je réflechis. 6. Nous ne comprenons pas. 7. Nous venons de perdre. 8. Choisissons! 9. Ralentissez! 10. Ne t'inquiète pas!

ADVERBS

assez – quite, fairly	peu – little, not much
très – very	vraiment – really
sans doute – doubtless	tellement – so, such a

Moi (m), je suis assez fatigué – I'm fairly tired
Il est peu disposé au travail – He's not inclined to work
Vous êtes très jolie, Mademoiselle – You're very pretty, miss
Vous êtes vraiment bizarre, Monsieur – You're really strange, sir
Elle est sans doute anglaise – No doubt she is English
Les Anglais sont tellement romantiques – The English are so romantic
Accepter plutôt que refuser – To accept rather than to refuse

ORDINAL NUMBERS

Ordinal numbers are regularly formed by adding *ième* to the cardinal number:

deuxième – second
vingtième – twentieth

dix-huitième – eighteenth
trente et unième – thirty-first

The irregular forms are:

premier – first   neuvième – ninth
second – second (alternative form) (SeGŌD)

au deuxième étage – on the second floor
au rez-de-chaussée – on the ground floor
au sous-sol – in the basement
voyager en seconde – to travel second class
être premier (m) en classe – to be top of the class (a boy)
les dix premières pages – the first ten pages

TOUT, TOUTE, TOUS, TOUTES – ALL, EVERY, THE WHOLE OF

tout le monde (+ sing. verb) – everybody
tout le temps – all the time
tous les jours – every day
tous les lundis – every Monday
elles y sont toutes – they (f) are all here
rien du tout – nothing at all
tout à l'heure – just now, in a minute
tout d'un coup – all of a sudden
tout de suite – straight away

LA MÉTÉO – WEATHER FORECAST

Quel temps fait-il? – What's the weather like?
Il fait beau – The weather's good
Il fait mauvais temps – The weather's bad
Il fait chaud, froid – It's warm, cold
Il fait du vent – It's windy
Il fait du brouillard – It's foggy

Il fait du soleil – It's sunny
un temps affreux, épouvantable – awful, terrible, weather
un temps lourd, sec, incertain – heavy, dry, changeable weather
se mettre au beau – to turn finer, to clear up
sortir par tous les temps – to go out in all weathers

slang ⎰ Ça flotte – It's raining
⎱ Ça caille – It's perishing cold

Word-building

neiger, il neige, la neige – to snow, it's snowing, snow
pleuvoir, il pleut, la pluie – to rain, it's raining, rain
geler, il gèle, la glace – to freeze, it's freezing, ice
dégeler, il dégèle, le dégel – to thaw, it's thawing, thaw
brumeux(se), la brume – misty, mist
nuageux(se), le nuage – cloudy, cloud
orageux(se), un orage – stormy, storm
frais (fraîche), se rafraîchir – cool, to turn chilly
doux (douce), se radoucir – mild, to turn mild
une éclaircie, s'éclaircir – sunny period, to brighten up
une averse, il pleut à verse – shower, it's pouring

Vocabulary

le ciel – sky
le reste – rest
le nord – north
le sud – south
l'est – east
l'ouest – west
la fin – end
l'ensemble – the whole
la température – temperature

isolé – isolated
ensoleillé – sunny
parisien(ne) – Parisian
belge – Belgian
prédominer – predominate
bénéficier de – to enjoy
ensemble – together
cependant – however
en hausse – higher
en baisse – lower

■ Translation

Le ciel va rester très nuageux sur la région parisienne. Le même type de temps va prédominer sur les régions qui s'étendent de la Loire à la frontière belge. Des éclaircies vont se produire cependant. Le reste de la France va bénéficier d'un temps ensoleillé, mais brumeux le matin au sud de la Loire. Quelques orages isolés vont se développer en fin de journée sur les Pyrénées, le nord des Alpes et la Corse.

Demain: le temps va être humide et assez chaud sur l'ensemble du pays, et les températures vont être plutôt en baisse.

La région parisienne: temps doux avec pluies ou averses orageuses et un vent d'est faible – températures en légère hausse.

The sky will remain very cloudy over the Paris area. The same type of weather will predominate over the area extending from the Loire to the Belgian border. Bright periods will, however, occur. The rest of France will enjoy sunny weather, but misty in the morning to the south of the Loire. A few isolated storms will develop at the end of the day over the Pyrenees, the northern Alps and Corsica.

Tomorrow: the weather will be humid and fairly warm over the whole of the country and the temperatures will be rather lower.

Paris area: mild weather with rain or stormy showers and a gentle east wind – temperatures slightly higher.

LESSON NINE

MODAL VERBS

Present tense

	vouloir – to wish or want	*savoir – to know (how to)*
je	veux	sais
tu	veux	sais
il	veut	sait
nous	voulons	savons
vous	voulez	savez
ils	veulent	savent
past p.:	voulu	su

	pouvoir – to be able to (e.g. I can, etc.)	devoir – to have to, must, ought to, to owe
je	peux (puis)	dois
tu	peux	dois
il	peut	doit
nous	pouvons	devons
vous	pouvez	devez
ils	peuvent	doivent
past p.:	pu	dû (f due)

Note: *puis* is a form used only in inversion: *puis-je*? – can I?
Modal verbs are usually followed by another verb in the infinitive.

Exercise

1. I want to go out. 2. He can (knows how to) play. 3. We can go in. 4. You (sing.) ought to know. 5. They (m) want to know how to dress. 6. Are you (pl) going to be able to come? 7. You have to pay. 8. I can't go.

1. Je veux sortir. 2. Il sait jouer. 3. Nous pouvons entrer. 4. Tu dois savoir. 5. Ils veulent savoir comment s'habiller. 6. Allez-vous pouvoir venir? 7. On doit payer. 8. Je ne peux pas y aller.

Verb usage

Je ne peux plus supporter ce mec – I can't stand that bloke any more
Il ne peut pas y avoir des . . . – There couldn't be any . . .
Ça ne se peut pas. Il se peut que . . . – That's impossible. It could be that . . .
Tu peux rester là si tu veux – You can stay there if you want
Je fais ce que je peux. Ça se peut – I'm doing what I can. Could be
Voulez-vous garder le silence! – Will you keep quiet!
Qu'est-ce que ça veut dire? – What does that mean?
Qu'est-ce que tu veux dire? – What do you mean?
Tu sais comment il s'appelle? – Do you know what he's called?
Savez-vous à quelle heure il va partir? – Do you know what time he's leaving?
Il ne sait pas conduire – He can't drive

Connaître = to know people places and subjects:
Tu connais des Français? Il connaît le français – Do you know any
  French people? He knows French.

Devoir means 'to owe', when used without an infinitive:

Combien je vous dois, Madame? – How much do I owe you,
  madam?

  With the infinitive, it means 'must', 'ought to':

Vous devez travailler si vous voulez réussir – You have to work if
  you're going to succeed
Il doit vous connaître – He must know you
Nous devons partir demain – We have to leave tomorrow

  Valoir means 'to be worth'. *Il vaut* . . . means 'it's worth . . .'

Ça ne vaut rien – It's worth nothing
Ça vaut le coup – It's worth it!
Ça vaut la peine – It's worth the trouble
C'est (ce n'est) pas la peine – It's not worth it!

  Veuillez is the imperative of *vouloir*. It is extremely polite and
formal:

Veuillez ne pas vous pencher au dehors – Kindly do not lean out
Veuillez vous asseoir – Kindly sit down

  Il faut + infinitive means 'must', 'have to', 'got to'

Il faut y aller – You (we) have to go
Il faut savoir – We've (you've) got to know

RELATIVE PRONOUN

ce qui – what, that (subject)   *ce que* – what, that (object)
ce dont – what (with a preposition, or if the verb does not take a
direct object).
dont means 'of' (or 'about') 'whom' (or 'which')
le train dont je vais me renseigner – the train about which I'm going
to inquire

REFLEXIVE USE OF TRANSITIVE VERBS

Comment se fait-il que vous êtes malade? – How is it that you're ill?
Comment ça se fait que . . . ? – How is it that . . . ?
Comment ça se dit en français? – How is that said in French?
Un film qui se voit avec plaisir – A film which people enjoy seeing
Ça se voit tous les jours – You can see that every day
Se mettre à faire quelque chose – to begin to do something

Note:

faire faire quelque chose – to have something done
faire enregistrer les bagages – to have the luggage registered
faire venir quelqu'un – to get someone to come
faire venir le médecin – to call the doctor
faire bouillir les pommes de terre – to boil the spuds

OBJECT PRONOUNS – DIRECT AND INDIRECT

Direct object   elle m'embrasse – she's kissing me
Indirect object   je lui montre le chemin – I show him (= to him)
                         the way

Subject	*Direct object*	*Indirect object*
je	me – me	me – to me
tu	te – you	te – to you
il	le – him, it	lui – to him, to it
elle	la – her, it	lui – to her, to it
reflexive	se – himself, etc.	se – to himself, etc.
nous	nous – us	nous – to us
vous	vous – you	vous – to you
ils	les – them	leur – to them
elles	les – them	leur – to them
reflexive	se – themselves	se – to themselves

Position

Object pronouns are placed immediately before the verb:

Je te donne mon adresse – I'm giving you (= to you) my address
Tu ne m'écoutes pas – You're not listening to me

Le voyez-vous? – Can you see him (it)?
Nous n'allons pas les trouver – We're not going to find them
Ne le faites pas – Don't do it

When two or more objects precede the same verb, they are put in this order:

1 me, te, se, nous, vous before	4 y (there) before
2 le, la, les before	5 en (of it, about it)
3 lui, leur before	

Exercise

1. You're (sing.) giving them to me. 2. He's not selling them to me. 3. I'm going to talk to you (pl) about it. 4. Don't send (pl) it to them. 5. You're (pl) missing some (There are some missing to you). 6. There aren't any. 7. He washes them there.

1. Tu me les donne. 2. Il ne me les vend pas. 3. Je vais vous en parler. 4. Ne le leur envoyez pas. 5. Il vous en manque. 6. Il n'y en a pas. 7. Il les y lave.

Pronouns in group (1) cannot appear together before the same verb. Instead, the indirect pronoun is changed to *à* + stressed pronoun and placed after the verb:

je m'intéresse à vous – I'm interested in you
ils se moquent de moi – they're laughing at me
adresse-toi à eux – speak to them

Object pronouns with *voici* and *voilà* precede:

les voilà! – there they are!   me voici! – here I am!

In the positive imperative, the pronoun follows the verb and a hyphen is added. *Moi* and *toi* replace the normal *me* and *te*. If there is more than one pronoun, the normal English order is followed:

prenez-les – take them
allez-y! – go on
donnez-les-moi – give them to me
envoyez-la-leur – send it to them
profitez-en – make use of it

La SNCF (La Société Nationale des Chemins de Fer Français) – FRENCH RAILWAYS

Vocabulary

la ligne – line	s'adresser à – to go to, speak to
un horaire – timetable (poster)	avertir – to warn
un indicateur – timetable (book)	consulter – to consult
le guichet – ticket-office	faire la queue – to queue up
une carte – card, map	réserver – to reserve
le fumeur – smoker	conseiller – to advise
le compartiment – compartment	risquer – to risk, might
la place – room, seat	prier – to request
la correspondance – connection	une carte d'abonnement (m) – season ticket
l'arrivée (f) – arrival	un billet simple – one way ticket
le départ – departure	un billet aller et retour – return ticket
le wagon-lit – sleeping-car	le demi-tarif – half-price
la couchette – couchette	en provenance (f) de – coming from
le chariot – trolley	à destination (f) de – going to
vite – quickly	
le retard – delay	
être à l'heure – to be on time	
le passager – passenger	
le quai – platform	

■ *Conversation*

'Le train en provenance de Bordeaux va arriver au quai numéro quatre à l'heure prévue, c'est à dire à dix-huit heures trente. Il y a un léger retard sur la ligne Paris–Lille. Les passagers à destination de Paris sont priés de s'adresser au bureau des renseignements. Nous avertissons mesdames et messieurs les voyageurs que le train en provenance de Bruxelles va partir pour Londres du quai numéro treize dans dix minutes . . .'

Fils: Ça y est, papa, je viens de trouver un chariot. À quelle heure part le train?

Père: Les horaires, je ne les comprends jamais. On va se renseigner au guichet. (Il met les valises sur le chariot et ils font la queue devant le guichet. Au bout de quelques instants . . .) Un billet pour Paris, combien coûte-t-il, monsieur?

Employé: Vous voulez un billet simple ou aller et retour? Un billet de quai? Un billet à demi-tarif? Une carte d'abonnement? Vous voulez réserver une couchette?

Père: Qu'est-ce qu'il dit? Je n'y comprends rien. Ils parlent si vite, ces Français.

Mère: Trois billets simples en second et deux autres à demi-tarif, s'il vous plaît.

Employé: Ça vous fait trois cent vingt francs, Madame.

Mère: À quelle heure est le premier départ pour Paris? Est-ce qu'il nous faut changer de train?

Employé: Il y en a toutes les demi-heures. À Amiens, il vous faut attendre la correspondance pour Paris. Je vous conseille d'être à l'heure parce qu'aujourd'hui il y a pas mal de monde qui descend sur Paris et vous risquez de ne pas trouver assez de place.

Mère: Allez, au revoir et merci, Monsieur.

Employé: De rien, Madame. Au revoir et bon voyage.

(Ils passent le contrôle, trouvent le quai d'embarquement, montent les valises dans le train et s'installent dans un compartiment 'Non-fumeurs'.)

'The train from Bordeaux will arrive at platform 4 on stated time (schedule), that is to say at 18.30. There is a slight delay on the Paris–Lille line. Passengers for Paris are requested to go to the information office. We warn passengers that the train from Brussels will leave for London from platform 13 in ten minutes . . .'

Son: There we are, Dad, I've just found a trolley. What time does the train leave?

Father: I never understand timetables. We shall make enquiries at the ticket-office. (He puts the cases on the trolley and they queue up in front of the ticket-office. After a few moments . . .) How much is a ticket to Paris?

Clerk: Do you want a single or return ticket? A platform ticket? A half-price ticket? A season ticket? Do you want to reserve a couchette?

Father: What's he saying? I can't understand it at all. These Frenchmen speak so fast.

Mother: Three second-class single tickets and two morc at half price, please.

Clerk: That makes 320 francs, madam.

Mother: What time is the first train to Paris? Do we have to change trains?

Clerk: There are trains every half-hour. At Amiens you have to wait for the connection for Paris. I advise you to be on time because there are a lot of people going to Paris today and you might not find enough seats.

Mother: Good-bye and thank you.

Clerk: Not at all, madam. Goodbye and have a good journey. (They go through the ticket barrier, find the departure platform, put the cases into the train and settle down in a non-smoking compartment.)

LESSON TEN

REMAINING IRREGULAR VERBS

Present tense

	A *ouvrir – to open*	B *dormir – to sleep*	C *courir – to run*
je(j')	ouvre	dors	cours
tu	ouvres	dors	cours
il	ouvre	dort	court
nous	ouvrons	dormons	courons
vous	ouvrez	dormez	courez
ils	ouvrent	dorment	courent
past p.:	ouvert	dormi	couru

	D *mourir – to die*	E *fuir – to flee*	F *conduire – to lead, drive*
je	meurs	fuis	conduis
tu	meurs	fuis	conduis
il	meurt	fuit	conduit
nous	mourons	fuyons	conduisons
vous	mourez	fuyez	conduisez
ils	meurent	fuient	conduisent
past p.:	mort	fui	conduit

	G *écire – to write*	**H** *suivre – to follow*	**J** *craindre – to fear*
je(j')	écris	suis	crains
tu	écris	suis	crains
il	écrit	suit	craint
nous	écrivons	suivons	craignons
vous	écrivez	suivez	craignez
ils	écrivent	suivent	craignent
past p.:	écrit	suivi	craint

	K *lire – to read*	**L** *rire – to laugh*	**M** *vivre – to live*
je	lis	ris	vis
tu	lis	ris	vis
il	lit	rit	vit
nous	lisons	rions	vivons
vous	lisez	riez	vivez
ils	lisent	rient	vivent
past p.:	lu	ri	vécu

	N *boire – to drink*	**O** *croire – to believe*	**P** *naître – to be born*
je	bois	crois	nais
tu	bois	crois	nais
il	boit	croit	naît
nous	buvons	croyons	naissons
vous	buvez	croyez	naissez
ils	boivent	croient	naissent
past p.:	bu	cru	né

	Q *s'asseoir – to sit down*	**R** *recevoir – to receive*	**S** *se taire – to be silent*
je	m'assieds	reçois	me tais
tu	t'assieds	reçois	te tais
il	s'assied	reçoit	se tait
nous	nous asseyons	recevons	nous taisons
vous	vous asseyez	recevez	vous taisez
ils	s'asseyent	reçoivent	se taisent
past p.:	assis	reçu	tu

Conjugated as above are:

A
couvrir – cover
découvrir – discover
offrir – offer
souffrir – suffer

B
s'endormir – go to sleep
mentir – (tell a) lie
partir – leave
sentir – feel
servir – serve
sortir – go out

E
s'enfuir – run away

F
réduire – reduce
construire – build
cuire – cook
détruire – destroy
instruire – instruct
produire – produce
traduire – translate

G
décrire – describe
s'inscrire – enrol

H
poursuivre – pursue, continue

J
atteindre – reach
éteindre – switch off
joindre – join
peindre – paint
plaindre – complain
rejoindre – join (someone)

K
relire – re-read

L
sourire

M
survivre – survive

R
apercevoir – notice
décevoir – deceive

Cueillir – to gather, pick, like the verbs in group A, has an *-ir* infinitive, but *-er* present tense verb endings. However, the past participle is *cueilli*. Note also: *accueillir* – to welcome.

Rompre – to break, follows *vendre* and is regular except for the 3rd person singular – *il rompt*. Note also: *interrompre* – to interrupt.

Battre – to beat, follows *vendre* except in the first three persons: *je bats, tu bats, il bat – nous battons, vous battez, ils battent.*

Exercise

1. I feel. 2. He's not going out. 3. You (sing.) offer me. 4. Let's run away! 5. We're destroying it. 6. Translate (pl). 7. We're not enrolling. 8. Follow (pl) me. 9. They switch off. 10. I fear it. 11. They are smiling. 12. Let's drink it. 13. Do you (pl) think so? 14. Sit down (pl). 15. Shut up! (pl). 16. We don't notice. 17. He's not leaving. 18. I'm going to sleep. 19. They (m) are fighting (each other). 20. We don't welcome them. 21. discovered. 22. painted. 23. cooked. 24. survived. 25. left.

1. Je sens. 2. Il ne sort pas. 3. Tu m'offres. 4. Enfuyons-nous! 5. Nous le détruisons. 6. Traduisez. 7. Nous ne nous inscrivons pas. 8. Suivez-moi. 9. Ils éteignent. 10. Je le crains. 11. Ils sourient. 12. Buvons-le. 13. Le croyez-vous? 14. Asseyez-vous. 15. Taisez-vous! 16. Nous n'apercevons pas. 17. Il ne part pas. 18. Je m'endors. 19. Ils se battent. 20. Nous ne les accueillons pas. 21. découvert. 22. peint. 23. cuit. 24. survécu. 25. parti.

■ PRONUNCIATION AND SPELLING VARIATIONS IN -ER VERBS (PRESENT TENSE)

Verbs ending in *-ger* and *-cer* maintain the soft sound before *o* and *a* by adding *e* or a cedilla ( ):
manger – to eat: nous mangeons
commencer – to begin: nous commençons

Verbs such as mener – to lead, acheter – to buy, se promener – to go for a walk, lever – to raise, geler – to freeze, emmener – to lead away
take a grave accent before mute endings:
mène, mènes, mène, menons, menez, mènent

Verbs such as répéter – to repeat   espérer – to hope
           posséder – to possess   protéger – to protect
change é to è before mute endings:
répète, répètes, répète, répétons, répétez, répètent

Verbs such as appeler – to call   jeter – to throw
double the consonant before mute endings:
jette, jettes, jette, jetons, jetez, jettent

Verbs such as ennuyer – to bore   essuyer – to wipe
           nettoyer – to clean   employer – to use
           envoyer – to send
change y to i before mute endings:
emploie, emploies, emploie, employons, employez, emploient
With payer – to pay, and essayer – to try, the change is optional.

■ *Pronunciation*

mangeons (MĀZHŌ))	mènent (MEN)	appelons (aPLŌ)
menons (MeNŌ)	jetons (ZHeTŌ)	appelle (aPEL)
espérer (eSPéRé)	jettes (ZHET)	emploie (ĀPLWa)
ennuyer (ĀNWiYé)	achète (aSHET)	espère (eSPER)
commencer (KoMĀSé)		

Verb usage

Je voudrais changer des livres en francs – I would like to change pounds for francs

dépanner un appareil de télévision – to repair a television set

Je commence *à* en avoir assez! – I'm beginning to have had enough!

avoir du mal *à* prononcer correctement un mot – to have difficulty in pronouncing a word correctly

jeter des projectiles du haut du toit – to throw things from the top of the roof

envoyer quelqu'un chercher la poste – to send someone to find the post office

allumer (éteindre) les phares – to switch on (off) the headlights remercier quelqu'un pour sa gentillesse – to thank someone for his kindness

s'assurer contre les accidents – to insure against accidents

être (ne pas être) d'accord – to agree (disagree)

EN ROUTE POUR PARIS – ON THE WAY TO PARIS

Vocabulary

un accélérateur – accelerator	brusquement – suddenly
une accélération – acceleration	drôle – funny
une auto – car	encombré – crowded
la bagnole (slang) – car	foudroyant – thundering
la ceinture – belt	grâce à – because of, thanks to
le chauffeur – driver	grave – serious
la circulation – traffic	heureusement – fortunately
le compteur – speedometer	sain – healthy
la dépanneuse – breakdown truck	sauf – safe
le frein – brake	appuyer – to lean
le moteur – engine	dépanner – to help out, fix
la panique – panic	éviter – to avoid
le plat – level, flat	freiner – to brake
la sécurité – safety	lâcher – to let go (of)
le virage – corner	marcher – to walk (to work, of machines)
la vitesse – speed, gear	mettre le contact – to switch on (ignition)
le volant – steering-wheel	ranger – to park, file

■ *Conversation*

Père: Vraiment je trouve qu'il est très facile de conduire en France, surtout parce qu'il y a très peu de circulation. Les routes ne sont jamais encombrées. Quand vous avez un chauffeur comme moi, on roule sans problèmes et à toute vitesse. Regardez le compteur! Cette voiture a des accélérations foudroyantes! (Il passe en troisième et appuie sur l'accélérateur.)

Fils: Mon copain a une bagnole qui est capable du cent soixante à l'heure sur le plat. Ce gars-là, il appuie vraiment sur le champignon.

(Papa, au volant, change les vitesses et passe en quatrième.)

Mère: Mais non, pas si vite, nom de Dieu! Il y a encore trois cents kilomètres pour aller à Paris. Tu vas rentrer dans un arbre! Attention à ce virage!

(Papa freine brusquement et donne un coup de volant. Il lâche l'accélérateur et range l'auto sur le bord de la route.)

Père: Elle freine bien, la voiture, n'est-ce pas? Elle a de bons freins. Grâce à moi, nous venons d'éviter un accident grave.

Mère: C'est les ceintures de sécurité qui viennent d'empêcher un accident. Ce n'est pas toi. Heureusement, nous sommes sains et saufs.

Père: Ça va derrière? Alors, on y va. Je vais mettre le contact.

(Silence pendant deux minutes.)

Fils: Qu'est-ce qu'il y a? Ça ne marche pas, le moteur? Ah, qu'est-ce que tu es drôle, papa, quand tu es fâché!

Père: Restez calme, tout le monde, pas de panique. Et, jeune homme, un peu de silence, s'il te plaît. Il y a un garage là-bas.

Fils: Est-ce qu'il y a un mécanicien qui va venir nous dépanner?

Mère: Ce n'est pas vrai! Nous allons arriver à Paris en dépanneuse!

Father: I really find it's easy to drive in France, especially because there's not much traffic. The roads are never crowded. When you have a driver like me, you travel without problems and at top speed. Look at the speedometer! This car has stunning acceleration! (He changes into third and accelerates.)

Son: My friend has a car which is capable (of doing) 160 km an hour (100 mph) on the flat. That guy, he really steps on the gas (lit.: 'leans on the mushroom').

(Dad, at the steering-wheel, changes gear and goes into top.)

Mother: Oh no, not so fast, for goodness sake! We've still got 300 km to go to Paris. You're going to pile into a tree. Look out for this corner!

(Dad brakes suddenly and pulls hard on the steering-wheel. He takes his foot off the accelerator and parks the car at the edge of the road).

Father: The car brakes well, doesn't it? It's got good brakes. Thanks to me, we have just avoided a serious accident.

Mother: It's the seat-belts that have just prevented an accident.

Colloquial French is also available in the form of a course pack (ISBN 0-415-03890-1), containing this book and an accompanying audio cassette. The pronunciation guide, exercises, conversations and idiomatic phrases contained in the book have been recorded by native speakers of French, making the cassette an invaluable aid to speaking and comprehension.

If you have been unable to obtain the course pack the cassette can be ordered separately through your bookseller or, in the case of difficulty, cash with order from Routledge Ltd, ITPS, Cheriton House, North Way, Andover, Hants SP10 5BE, price £8.99* including VAT, or from Routledge, Chapman and Hall Inc., 29 West 35th Street, New York, NY 10001, USA

For your convenience an order form is attached.

**The publishers reserve the right to change prices without notice*

CASSETTE ORDER

Please supply one/two/ . . . . . cassette(s) of

Humphreys, *Colloquial French*
ISBN 0-415-03889-8
Price £8.99 inc. VAT

☐ I enclose payment with order.

☐ Please debit my Access/Mastercharge/Visa/American Express account number

Expiry date ....

Name ....

Address ....

....

Order to your bookseller or to . . .

ROUTLEDGE LTD
ITPS
Cheriton House
North Way
Andover
Hants
SP10 5BE
ENGLAND

ROUTLEDGE INC.
29 West 35th Street
New York
NY 10001
USA

It's not you. Fortunately we are safe and sound (lit.: 'healthy and safe').

Father: OK behind? Off we go, then. I'm going to switch on. (Silence for two minutes.)

Son: What's wrong? Doesn't the engine work? Ah, how funny you are, Dad, when you're angry!

Father: Stay calm, everybody. Don't panic. And, young man, a little silence, please. There's a garage over there.

Son: Is there a mechanic who's going to come and help out?

Mother: I don't believe it! We're going to arrive in Paris in a breakdown truck!

LESSON ELEVEN

PAST PARTICIPLE

Regular

donner – donné (given)
finir – fini (finished)
vendre – vendu (sold)

aller – allé (gone)
remplir – rempli (filled)
entendre – entendu (understood)

Irregular

Verb groups A – S in the last chapter introduced most of the irregular forms. Turn back and learn them. Other irregularities are:

acquérir, acquis (acquired)
avoir, eu (had)
connaître, connu (known)
devoir, dû (owed)
dire, dit (said)
être, été (been)
faire, fait (done)
il faut, fallu (had to)
mettre, mis (put)
paraître, paru (appeared)

pleuvoir, plu (rained)
pouvoir, pu (been able)
prendre, pris (taken)
savoir, su (known)
tenir, tenu (held)
vaincre, vaincu (defeated)
valoir, valu (been worth)
venir, venu (come)
voir, vu (seen)
vouloir, voulu (wanted)

PERFECT TENSE

Avoir

The perfect tense is formed with the present tense of an auxiliary verb and the past participle; the auxiliary verb may be *avoir* or *être*.

Most verbs form their perfect tense with *avoir*:

{ I have given { I gave	{ I didn't finish { I haven't finished	{ have I sold? { did I sell?
j'ai donné	je n'ai pas fini	ai-je vendu?
tu as donné	tu n'as pas fini	as-tu vendu?
il a donné	il n'a pas fini	a-t-il vendu?
nous avons donné	nous n'avons pas fini	avons-nous vendu?
vous avez donné	vous n'avez pas fini	avez-vous vendu?
ils ont donné	ils n'ont pas fini	ont-ils vendu?
n'ai-je pas donné?	n'ai-je pas fini?	n'ai-je pas vendu?

Être

A small group of verbs of movement and change of condition are conjugated with *être*. Learn them in pairs:

aller	venir	go	come
revenir	devenir	come back	become
partir	sortir	leave	go out
monter	descendre	go up	go down
arriver	rester	arrive	stay
entrer	rentrer	go in	go home
retourner	tomber	return	fall
naître	mourir	be born	die

Je suis allé(e) – I went   Il est venu – He's come   Tu n'es pas sorti(e) – You didn't go out   Sont-ils morts? – Are they dead?

Être itself is conjugated with *avoir*:

J'ai été – I was   Nous avons été – we were

Reflexive verbs

All reflexive verbs form the perfect tense with *être*:

I've washed } I washed }	Have I washed? } did I wash? }

je me suis lavé(e)	me suis-je lavé(e)?
tu t'es lavé(e)	t'es-tu lavé(e)?
il s'est lavé	s'est-il lavé?
nous nous sommes lavé(e)s	nous sommes-nous lavé(e)s?
vous vous êtes lavé(e)s	vous êtes-vous lavé(e)s?
ils se sont lavés	se sont-ils lavés?
je ne me suis pas lavé(e)	il ne s'est pas lavé
ne me suis-je pas lavé(e)?	ne s'est'il pas lavé?

Object pronoun – position

The object pronoun always comes immediately before the auxiliary:

je l'ai fait – I did it
tu lui as dit – you told him (or her)
il le leur a montré – he showed it to them

AGREEMENT OF PAST PARTICIPLE

The past participle is really an adjective:

vendu (m), vendue (f), vendus (m pl), vendues (f pl)

But what does it agree with?

When avoir is used

The past participle agrees only with a preceding direct object. For there to be agreement, the object must be direct and must precede the verb:

Example	*Object?*	*Direct?*	*Preceding?*	*Agreement?*
Il a fait	NO	—	—	—
elle a fait la vaisselle	YES	YES	NO	NO
la porte, je l'ai ouverte	YES	YES	YES	YES
les mots que tu as dits	YES	YES	YES	YES
elle leur a vendu	YES	NO	YES	NO
ils en ont parlé	YES	NO	YES	NO
je les ai essayés	YES	YES	YES	YES

In verbs of movement

These verbs are intransitive and cannot take a direct object. Instead, the past participle agrees with the subject:

ils sont arrivés – they (m) arrived
elle est morte – she died
ma mère est venue me voir – my mother came to see me
nos copines sont parties – our friends (f) have left

In reflexive verbs

The reflexive pronoun is the direct object in verbs involving 'doing something to oneself', such as *se laver* – to wash. The past participle agrees with the reflexive pronoun:

ils se sont comportés – they behaved (themselves)
elle s'est cachée – she hid (herself)

When the reflexive pronoun is an indirect object, there is no agreement:

ils se sont écrit – they wrote (to each other)
elle s'est demandé – she wondered (asked *to* herself)

Reference table – perfect tense

| | Conjugation | | Agreement | | |
	être	avoir	prec. dir. object	subject	reflexive pronoun
Movement verbs	YES	—	—	YES	—
Reflexive (doing to oneself)	YES	—	—	—	YES
Reflexive (doing to each other)	YES	—	—	—	—
All other verbs	—	YES	YES	—	—

Exercise

1. We said. 2. I knew. 3. You (sing.) have seen. 4. Did he drink? 5. She didn't lie. 6. He fell asleep. 7. I wasn't. 8. We've had. 9. Hasn't he come back? 10. You (m pl) didn't leave. 11. I was worried. 12. They (f) shook hands. 13. She took the train. 14. We saw them (m). 15. You (sing.) showed me. They (m) defeated us (m). 17. I discovered you (f sing.). 18. He made fun of me. 19. She knew us (m). 20. We wanted some.

1. Nous avons dit. 2. J'ai su. 3. Tu as vu. 4. A-t-il bu? 5. Elle n'a pas menti. 6. Il s'est endormi. 7. Je n'ai pas été. 8. Nous avons eu. 9. N'est-il pas revenu? 10. Vous n'êtes pas partis. 11. Je me suis inquiété(e). 12. Elles se sont serré la main. 13. Elle a pris le train. 14. Nous les avons vus. 15. Tu m'as montré. 16. Ils nous ont vaincus. 17. Je t'ai découvert(e). 18. Il s'est moqué de moi. 19. Elle nous a connus. 20. Nous en avons voulu.

Verb usage

Monter, *descendre*, *sortir*, *rentrer* have a second, transitive, meaning and in this sense take *avoir*:

j'ai monté les bagages – I took the luggage up
il a descendu ses affaires – he brought his things down
sortez vos papiers, s'il vous plaît – take your papers out, please
j'ai rentré mes livres à la bibliothèque – I took my books back to the
    library

COMPARISON OF ADJECTIVES

Positive	haut – high
Comparative	plus haut – higher
Superlative	le plus haut – highest

Superlatives

les plus grands légumes – the biggest vegetables
les choses les plus difficiles – the most difficult things

The possessive adjective, with a superlative standing before the noun, replaces the definite article:

mon plus joli tableau – my prettiest picture
mes plus belles plantes – my most beautiful plants

But when the adjective follows the noun, the definite article is needed:

son histoire la plus intéressante – his, her, most interesting story
nos parents les plus riches – our richest relations

Exceptions

These adjectives change their form and do not need *plus* and *le plus*:

bon – good	mauvais – bad	petit – small
meilleur – better	pire – worse	moindre – less(er)
le meilleur – best	le pire – worst	le moindre – least

Petit and *mauvais* can also be compared in the normal way:

petit, plus petit, le plus petit
mauvais, plus mauvais, le plus mauvais

Note these slight differences in meaning:

sans la moindre excuse – without the slightest excuse
les plus petites pommes – the smallest apples
la pire corruption – the worst corruption (moral)
le plus mauvais temps – the worst weather (physical)

Notice also: beaucoup, plus, le plus – a lot, more, most; and that *ne* is inserted after a comparison depending on a verb:
il est plus gourmand qu'il *ne* semble – he's greedier than he seems

Other comparisons

aussi gentille *que* ma tante – as nice as my aunt
moins jolie *que* ma soeur – not as (less . . . than) pretty as my sister
il est *plus* riche *que* moi – he's richer than me
il n'est pas *si* fort *que* toi – he's not as strong as you
la *plus* grande maison *de* la ville – the largest house in the town

l'habitant *le plus* vieux *du* village – the oldest inhabitant in the
   village
une leçon *très* (fort) difficile – a very difficult lesson
pâle *comme* la mort – as pale as death
doux *comme* un agneau – as gentle as a lamb
il est *plus* intelligent *que* tu *ne* penses – he's more intelligent than
   you think
tout le monde n'en a pas *autant* – not everyone has so many

FORMATION OF ADVERBS FROM ADJECTIVES

Adverbs of manner are regularly formed by adding *ment* to the
feminine singular of the adjective:

doux, douce – doucement – softly, sweetly
grand, grande – grandement – greatly

   If the adjective already ends in a vowel, then add *ment* to the
masculine:

vrai – vraiment – really, truly
poli – poliment – politely

Note:
énorme, énormément – enormously
profond, profondément – deeply
précis, précisément – precisely
aveugle, aveuglément – blindly
évident, évidemment (éViDaMĀ) – obviously
courant, couramment – fluently
gai, gaiement – gaily
bon, bien – well
mauvais, mal – badly

COMPARISON OF ADVERBS

Adverbs are compared in the same way as adjectives:

vite – quickly	lentement – slowly
plus vite – more quickly	plus lentement – more slowly
le plus vite – most quickly	le plus lentement – most slowly

Irregular

bien – well	peu – little	beaucoup – a lot
mieux – better	moins – less	plus – more
le mieux – best	le moins – least	le plus – most

C'est lui qui roule le plus vite – He's the one who drives fastest
Mais moi, je roule aussi vite que lui – But I drive as fast as him
Il parle moins poliment que sa mère – He speaks less politely than
   his mother
Plus il travaille, moins il mange – The more he works, the less he
   eats
Moins il mange, plus il gagne – The less he eats, the more he earns

Position of adverbs

Adverbs are never placed between subject and verb, as in English.
They usually follow the verb, although, for emphasis, they can begin
a sentence:

Nous mangeons souvent des frites – We often eat chips
Mais parfois nous achetons des chips – But sometimes we buy crisps
Il a énormément d'ennuis – He has tremendous problems
Nous y allons quelquefois – Sometimes we go there
Ça arrive de plus en plus – That happens more and more
Il se passe de moins en moins d'accidents – Fewer and fewer
   accidents take place

Plus de – more, and *moins de* – less, are used only with quan-
tities:

plus de vingt kilometres à faire – more than 20 km to go (do)
moins de vingt mille balles à gagner – less than 200 F to be won

À L'HÔTEL – AT THE HOTEL

Une lettre

Monsieur
Veuillez me retenir une chambre avec salle de bains, à grand lit
pour le 30 janvier. Je voudrais une chambre au rez-de-chaussée
donnant sur la mer. Nous espérons arriver dans la soirée vers six

heures et nous désirons dîner à l'hôtel. Nous allons rester trois nuits jusqu'au matin du 2 février.

Dans l'attente de votre confirmation, je vous prie d'agréer mes sentiments les plus distingués.

P. Morris

■ **Une conversation**

Bonsoir, Monsieur, je vous ai écrit il y a un mois pour réserver une chambre à deux personnes.

A quel nom?

Mon nom est Morris.

C'est ça. Je vous ai donné la chambre vingt. Voilà la clef, Monsieur. Je vais faire monter vos bagages.

C'est à quelle heure, le repas du soir et le petit déjeuner?

Le dîner, c'est au restaurant de dix-neuf heures à vingt heures trente. Vous pouvez prendre le petit déjeuner de sept heures trente jusqu'à neuf heures.

Vous avez un ascenseur?

Oui, Monsieur. Mais vous n'en avez pas besoin. Vous avez demandé une chambre au rez-de-chaussée, n'est-ce pas? Avant de monter à votre chambre, voulez-vous remplir cette fiche, s'il vous plaît . . . Je vous remercie. Bon séjour à Monte Carlo, Monsieur!

Letter

Dear Sir,

Would you kindly reserve me a room with bath and double bed for 30 January. I should like a room on the ground floor looking out over the sea. We hope to arrive about 6 in the evening and we would like dinner (at the hotel). We shall stay three nights until the morning of 2 February.

I look forward to your confirming this arrangement.

Yours faithfully (lit.: I beg you to accept my best wishes),

P. Morris

Conversation

Good evening. I wrote to you a month ago to reserve a room for two people.

In what name?

My name is Morris.

That's right. I have given you room 20. Here's the key, sir. I will have your luggage taken up.

What time are dinner and breakfast?

Dinner is in the restaurant from 7 to 8.30. You can have breakfast from 7.30 till 9.

Do you have a lift?

Yes, sir. But you don't need it. You asked for a room on the ground floor, didn't you? Before going to your room, would you please fill in this form . . . Thank you. Have a good stay in Monte Carlo, sir!

LESSON TWELVE

IMPERFECT TENSE

The imperfect is the tense of past description. It translates the English 'was doing', 'used to do' or 'did'.

To form the imperfect, take off the -ons from the 1st person plural of the present tense. This gives the stem. To this add the imperfect endings, which are the same for all verbs:

-ais, -ais, -ait, -ions, -iez, -aient

	donner	*finir*	*faire*
	nous donn(+ons)	nous finiss(+ons)	nous fais(+ons)
je	donnais	finissais	faisais
tu	donnais	finissais	faisais
il	donnait	finissait	faisait
nous	donnions	finissions	faisions
vous	donniez	finissiez	faisiez
ils	donnaient	finissaient	faisaient

The exception is *être*:

étais, étais, était, étions, étiez, étaient

Exercise

1. I was going. 2. We used to drink. 3. We didn't know him. 4. It

wasn't snowing. 5. They (m) used to be able to. 6. You (sing.) believed. 7. Did you (pl) know? 8. They (f) wanted. 9. I had to. 10. He was called.

1. J'allais. 2. Nous buvions. 3. Nous ne le connaissions pas. 4. Il ne neigeait pas. 5. Ils pouvaient. 6. Tu croyais. 7. Saviez-vous? 8. Elles voulaient. 9. Je devais. 10. Il s'appelait.

Uses of the imperfect

To describe a state of affairs existing in the past:

Il faisait froid – It was cold
J'étais toujours malade – I was always ill

To describe an action taking place when something else happened:

Elle regardait la télévision quand je suis entré – She was watching television when I came in

To describe habitual actions in the past:

Il se levait tous les matins à sept heures trente – He used to get up every morning at 7.30.

To translate 'would' (meaning 'used to'):

Mon père ne fumait jamais le matin – My father would never smoke in the morning

Imperfect and perfect tenses contrasted

The imperfect is used for description, the perfect for events. Note the tenses used in the following passage:

Nous habitions ce village depuis un an. Rien ne se passait là. Rien ne se passait jamais. C'était un soir en hiver. On était au mois de décembre. Il faisait déjà nuit. J'étais tout seul. Je me suis endormi dans le fauteuil. Au milieu de la nuit, je ne sais pas à quelle heure, vers une heure du matin peut-être, je me suis réveillé en sursaut. Je me suis demandé d'abord si ce n'était pas un prolongement de mon rêve. J'ai jeté un regard vers la fenêtre. Mais il n'y avait personne. Puis, soudain . . . (complete this story)

We had been living in that village for a year. Nothing happened there. Nothing ever happened. It was one evening in winter. It was in the month of December. It was already dark. I was all alone. I fell asleep in the armchair. In the middle of the night, I don't know what time, about one o'clock perhaps, I woke up with a jump. I wondered at first if it wasn't a continuation of my dream. I glanced towards the window. But there was nobody there. Then suddenly . . .

POSSESSIVE PRONOUNS

Masc.	Fem.	Masc. plural	Fem. plural	Meaning
le mien	la mienne	les miens	les miennes	mine
le tien	la tienne	les tiens	les tiennes	yours
le sien	la sienne	les siens	les siennes	his, hers, its
	le/la nôtre		les nôtres	ours
	le/la vôtre		les vôtres	yours
	le/la leur		les leurs	theirs

The gender depends on the thing possessed, not on the sex of the owner.

Cette voiture est la sienne – That car is his/hers
C'est à vous, cette valise? – Is this case yours?
Oui, oui, c'est la mienne – Yes, yes, it's mine
À la tienne! (la santé) – Good health (lit.: 'to yours')

Translate

It's mine. No, it's not, it's mine, I assure you. It's not yours, give it to me. No, will you give it to me! For the last time, it's mine. It's ours, and we're going to eat it. Too late. But it was mine.

C'est le mien. Mais non, c'est le mien, je vous assure. Ce n'est pas le vôtre, donnez-le-moi. Non, voulez-vous me le donner! Pour la dernière fois, c'est le mien. C'est le nôtre et nous allons le manger. Trop tard. Mais c'était le mien.

■ DATES

Les mois – months

All names of months are masculine and have no initial capital:

janvier	février	mars	avril
mai	juin	juillet	août
septembre	octobre	novembre	décembre

le premier juin, *le* deux avril, *le* dix septembre – on the first of June, on the second of April, on the tenth of September.

le vingt-cinq décembre – on 25th December

> Note: with *le huit* and *le onze*, no elision is made.

en mai, au mois de mai – in May
un beau jour de juillet - one fine day in July

Les ans – years

In dates, the form *mil* is used instead of *mille*:

En mil neuf cent soixante-dix-neuf (or en dix-neuf cent soixante-dix-neuf) – in 1979

le vingt janvier mil neuf cent quatre-vingts – 20 January 1980
les événements de mai soixante-huit – the events of May '68
au vingtième siècle – in the twentieth century

Translate

23/8/76, 14/12/79, 18/3/66, 1/1/87, in the sixteenth century, on the 4th of July.

DIMENSIONS

The following examples show another use of *avoir*:

Le bateau a vingt mètres de long – The boat is 20 m long
Cette route a cinq mètres de large – This road is 5 m wide
La rivière a une profondeur de dix mètres – This river is 10 m deep
Le bâtiment a quarante mètres de haut – The building is 40 m high

Ce gâteau a une épaisseur de trois centimètres – This cake is 3 cm thick

La ferme a une superficie de trois cents hectares – The farm has an area of 300 hectares

Cette église a cent mètres de long sur cent cinquante mètres de large – This church is 100 m long by 150 m wide

trois pieds carrés, deux cents mètres carrés – 3 square feet, 200 square metres

un bon kilomètre – at least 1 km

un petit kilomètre – barely, only about 1 km

PARTITIVE ARTICLE – ADJECTIVES (See pp. 28–9)

Before preceding plural adjectives, the partitive article is simply *de*:

de hautes montagnes – high mountains
de pareilles histoires – stories like this
d'autres fois – other times

If the adjective follows the noun, the normal rules apply:

des poissons frais – fresh fish
des cadeaux chers – expensive presents

The above rule is broken only in a few cases where the adjective and noun are so commonly found together that they almost form one word:

des jeunes filles – girls
des petits pois – peas
des grandes personnes – grown-ups
des petits pains – bread rolls

Verb usage

Placer + preposition can be replaced by the following verbs:
(*placer*)   contre (against) quelque chose = coller (to stick)
au dessus de (over) = couvrir (to cover)
plus bas (lower) = baisser (to lower)
plus haut (higher) = élever (to raise)
verticalement (vertically) = dresser (to stand)

plus près (nearer) = rapprocher (to bring nearer)
plus loin (farther) = éloigner (to move away)
à plat (flat) = étendre (to lay out)
entre (between) = interposer (to interpose)
ensemble (together) = joindre (to join)
en face (opposite) = opposer (to put opposite)
en ordre (in order) = arranger (to tidy up)

EN PANNE SUR LA ROUTE DE PARIS – UNE TENTATIVE DE RÉPARATION
BROKEN DOWN ON THE ROAD TO PARIS – AN ATTEMPT AT REPAIR

Vocabulary

un agent – policeman
l'assistance (f) – help
le bouchon – traffic jam
le capot – bonnet
le carburateur – carburettor
le coffre – boot (of car)
la courroie de ventilateur – fan-belt
le défaut – fault
un essuie-glace – windscreen wiper
les feux (m) de stationnement (m) – side-lights
le garagiste – garage hand
le hasard – chance
l'huile (f) – oil
le jet d'eau (f) – fountain, jet
le klaxon – horn
le lave-glace – windscreen washer
une offre – offer
le pare-brise – windscreen

le pneu – tyre
le policier – policeman
le radiateur – radiator
la remorque – trailer
la réparation – repair
le stationnement – parking
la tache – spot, stain
le tourchon – rag, duster
la tournure – twist, turn
le tuyau d'échappement – exhaust pipe
la voie – lane, line
circuler – to flow, move
se dégonfler – to deflate
détourner – to divert
se garer – to park
interdire – to forbid
vidanger (l'huile) – to change (the oil)
en tout cas – in any case
huileux(se) – oily

■ *Conversation*

Fils: Voilà qu'il arrive, le garagiste. Il est venu nous dépanner, papa.

Père: Ce n'est pas la peine. Je suis tout à fait dans mon élément avec les moteurs.

Garagiste: Bonjour, Messieurs, Dames. Je suis à votre service. Vous avez besoin d'un coup de main? (Il serre la main à tout le monde.) Oh, je m'excuse, j'ai les mains très sales. (Il s'essuie les mains avec un torchon, mais il est trop tard. Le fils a déjà laissé des taches d'huile sur le pare-brise.)

Père: On a quelques ennuis avec le moteur, mais ce n'est pas grave. Je suis sûr qu'il n'y a rien de grave. Je vous remercie de votre offre d'assistance. (Il regarde sous le capot, hésite une seconde et enfin commence à frapper des coups violents sur le carburateur.) Sûrement, c'est ce machin-là qui ne marche pas. On va être obligé de vidanger l'huile.

(Il frappe encore une fois. Le radiateur se casse en deux, le tuyau d'échappement et la courroie de ventilateur tombent par terre, en même temps que le lave-glaces envoie un jet d'eau sur le pare-brise. Silence pendant que tout le monde écoutent les pneus avant, qui commencent à se dégonfler lentement.)

Garagiste: Vous pensez que vous allez bientôt réussir à trouver le défaut, Monsieur? Reposez-vous un instant; ne vous pressez pas. C'est peut-être le klaxon ou les essuie-glaces qui ne fonctionnent pas? Vous êtes assuré? Ça va être beaucoup plus facile si vous êtes assuré. Mais allez-y! Vous travaillez vraiment comme un professionel.

(Un agent de police arrive en moto. Il n'est pas tellement content.)

Fils: Il y a un policier qui arrive, papa. Voilà qu'il arrive!

Policier: Allez, circulez, Monsieur! Ne restez pas là avec votre voiture. Il y a un énorme bouchon de circulation. Ici, le stationnement est interdit. Il est défendu de se garer sur l'autoroute.

Père: Les choses ont commencé à prendre une mauvaise tournure. (Il donne un coup de pied au coffre.) J'ai du mal à faire démarrer la voiture, Monsieur. Vous n'êtes pas mécanicien, par hasard?

Policier: Vite, vite, rentrez l'auto à la station-service. Vous interrompez la circulation sur une voie. Vraiment ça circule aujourd'hui. Je vais détourner tout le monde.

Père: Mais que faire?

Garagiste: Je suis à votre service, Monsieur. D'abord, allumez les feux de stationnement. Je vais chercher la dépanneuse et nous allons prendre l'auto en remorque. Une fois arrivés à la station-service, vous pouvez laisser la voiture chez nous et continuer votre voyage par le train. D'accord?

Mère: Ah, comment agir maintenant? Qu'est-ce que nous allons faire? Allons-nous jamais arriver à Paris?

Son: Here comes the man from the garage. He's coming to get us out of a spot, dad.

Father: It's not worth it. I'm quite at home with engines.

Garage man: Good afternoon, everyone. I'm at your service. Do you need a hand? (He shakes hands with everybody.) Oh, I'm sorry, my hands are very dirty. (He cleans his hands with a rag, but it's too late. Son has already left oily marks on the windscreen.)

Father: We have a few problems with the engine, but it's not serious. I'm sure there's nothing seriously wrong. Thank you for your offer of assistance. (He looks under the bonnet, hesitates for a second and finally begins to strike violent blows on the carburettor.) It's certainly this thing which doesn't work. We're going to have to change the oil.

(He hits once again. The radiator breaks in two, the exhaust pipe and the fan-belt fall to the ground, at the same time as the windscreen washers send a jet of water on to the windscreen. Silence while everyone listens to the front tyres, which are beginning to deflate slowly.)

Garage man: Do you think you'll soon succeed in finding the fault, sir? Have a rest for a moment; don't hurry. Perhaps it's the horn or the wipers which aren't working? Are you insured? It's going to be a lot easier if you are insured. But carry on! You're really working like a professional.

(A policeman arrives on a motorbike. He's not terribly happy.)

Son: There's a policeman coming, dad. Here he comes!

Policeman: Go on, keep moving! You can't park your car there. There's an enormous traffic jam. Parking is forbidden here. It's forbidden to park on the motorway.

Father: Things have begun to take a turn for the worse. (He gives the boot of the car a kick.) I'm having trouble starting the car, sir. You aren't a mechanic by any chance?

Policeman: Quick, hurry up and take the car back to the service station. You're holding up the traffic in one lane. There's really a lot of traffic today. I'm going to divert everyone.

Father: But what are we going to do?

Garage man: I'm at your service, sir. First, put on your side-lights. I'm going to fetch the breakdown truck and we'll take the car in tow. Once back at the service station you can leave your car with us and continue your journey by train. OK?

Mother: Ah, what shall we do now? What are we going to do? Will we ever get to Paris?

LESSON THIRTEEN

FUTURE TENSE

The future endings (-*ai*, -*as*, -*a*, -*ons*, -*ez*, -*ont*) are added to the infinitive of regular verbs:

donner   – donner+ai – je donnerai – I shall give
finir   – finir+as – tu finiras – you will finish
vendr(e) – vendr+a – il vendra – he will sell
se laver – laver+ont – ils se laveront – they will wash

Note that verbs in -*re* drop the final *e*:

croire   – croir+ons – nous croirons – we shall believe
lire   – lir+ez – vous lirez – you will read

All verbs have the same future endings. A few verbs have irregular future stems:

être (be) – je ser+ai   voir (see) – je verr+ai
avoir (have) – j'aur+ai   pleuvoir (rain) – il pleuvr+a
pouvoir (can) – je pourr+ai   recevoir (receive) – je recevr+ai
savoir (know) – je saur+ai   apercevoir (notice) –
                                     j'apercevr+ai

vouloir (want) – je voudr+ai   s'asseoir (sit down) – je
                                           m'assiér+ai

devoir (ought) – je devr+ai   il faut (have to) – il faudr+ai

Exercise: change into the future:

1. Nous buvons. 2. Tu sers. 3. Nous changeons. 4. Je sors. 5. Ils
veulent. 6. Elle a pris. 7. Je suis né. 8. Il permettait. 9. Vous vous
endormiez. 10. Écrivons-nous? 11. Elles ne savent pas. 12. Tu as
été. 13. Il s'est assis. 14. J'ai vu. 15. Vous avez. 16. Elle ouvre. 17.
Nous connaissons. 18. Tu romps. 19. Ils traduisaient. 20 Vous craig-
niez.

1. Nous boirons. 2. Tu serviras. 3. Nous changerons. 4. Je sortirai.
5. Ils voudront. 6. Elle prendra. 7. Je naîtrai. 8. Il permettra. 9.
Vous vous endormirez. 10. Écrirons-nous? 11. Elles ne sauront pas.
12. Tu seras. 13. Il s'assiéra. 14. Je verrai. 15. Vous aurez. 16. Elle
ouvrira. 17. Nous connaîtrons. 18. Tu rompras. 19. Ils traduiront.
20. Vous craindrez.

Use of the future

After conjunctions of time, the future tense is used when the sense is
future:

Quand j'aurai fini le repas, je sortirai avec toi – When I (shall) have
    finished the meal, I will go out with you
Dès que j'aurai passé la frontière, je serai en Belgique – As soon as
    I (shall) have crossed the border, I shall be in Belgium
Je le verrai lorsqu'il sera de retour – I shall see him when he gets
    (will get) back.

When 'will' or 'shall' expresses intention, use *vouloir*:

Il ne veut pas payer ses impôts – He will not pay his income tax
Voulez-vous vous asseoir! – Will you sit down!

Remember that the immediate future is commonly used in conversation:

Vous allez prendre le métro? Non, je vais plutôt y aller à pied – Are
    you going to take the tube? No, I'd rather go on foot

Note: être sur le point de – to be about to:

Le train était déjà sur le point de partir – The train was already on the point of leaving.

Exercise

1. We shall arrive in the afternoon. 2. Will you (pl) be at home tomorrow? 3. We'll drop in then at your house at that time. 4. Will you come with us? We'll gladly take you. 5. We'll tell him that you (sing.) will buy the present.

1. Nous arriverons dans l'après-midi. 2. Serez-vous chez vous demain? 3. Nous passerons donc chez vous à cette heure. 4. Voulez-vous venir avec nous? Nous vous emmenerons très volontiers. 5. Nous lui dirons que tu achèteras le cadeau.

Verb usage

Il faut without another verb means 'to be missing, lacking, to need'. Its English subject is the French dative pronoun:

Il me faut du temps – I need some time
Qu'est-ce qu'il me faut? – What do I need?
Il te faut de la chance – You need some luck

Followed by another verb in the infinitive, it means 'must, to have to':

Il faut travailler sans arrêt – You must work without a break
Il ne faut jamais vous demander pourquoi – You must never ask yourself why
Il nous faut rester chez nous – We have to stay at home
Il ne faut pas le faire – You mustn't do it
Il faut le faire – You have to do it

IMPERSONAL VERBS

Il y a des voitures et des voitures – There are cars and cars
Il reste du pain et du fromage – There's some bread and cheese left
Il n'en *reste* que trois – There are only three left

Qu'est-ce qui *se passe*? – What's happening?
Il se passe que je suis ennuyé – I'm bored, that's what happening
Parfois *il arrive* des accidents – Sometimes accidents happen
Il paraît que tu as eu de la chance – It seems that you were lucky
Il vaut mieux rester chez soi – You're better off staying at home
De quoi *s'agit-il*? – What's it all about?
Il s'agissait d'un meurtre – It was a question of murder

PRESENT PARTICIPLE

Formation

This is the '-ing' form of the verb: doing, going, eating. It is formed
by taking the *-ons* ending from the 1st person plural of the present
tense. To this is added, for all verbs, *-ant*.

nous donnons	donn+ant – giving
nous finissons	finiss+ant – finishing
nous vendons	vend+ant – selling
nous faisons	fais+ant – doing
nous mangeons	mange+ant – eating

Irregular

être	étant – being
avoir	ayant – having
savoir	sachant – knowing

Translate

1. believing. 2. gathering. 3. reading. 4. saying. 5. taking. 6.
opening. 7. seeing. 8. feeling. 9. promising. 10. producing.

1. croyant. 2. cueillant. 3. lisant. 4. disant. 5. prenant. 6. ouvrant. 7.
voyant. 8. sentant. 9. promettant. 10. produisant.

Usage

As an adjective, when it agrees with the noun:

des soucoupes volantes – flying saucers

elle est bien portante – she's well
l'eau bouillante – boiling water

As a verb, when it is invariable:

Elle était à l'aise, fumant une cigarette – She was relaxed, smoking a
   cigarette
Une fenêtre donnant sur la rue – A window looking out over the
   road

With *en*, when it is invariable:

En disant au revoir, elle a éclaté en sanglots – While saying
   goodbye, she burst into tears
En chantant ainsi, vous allez épouvanter votre mère – By singing
   like that, you will horrify your mother
En voyant le président, il a poussé des cris de joie – On seeing the
   president, he shouted out joyfully

When used with *en*, it can refer only to the *subject* of a sentence:

Je l'ai vu en mangeant des frites – I saw him when *I* was eating
   chips

Since 'he' is the object, we should say:

Je l'ai vu manger des frites – I saw *him* eating chips

Tout . . . en is used when two actions occur simultaneously:

Il conduisait la voiture tout en lisant le journal – He was driving the
   car while reading the paper.

Remember that 'I am giving' is the simple present tense: *je donne*.

Postures are expressed in French by the *past* participle:

assis – sitting	accroupi – squatting
agenouillé – kneeling	penché – leaning
couché – lying	accroché à – hanging on
appuyé – leaning	suspendu de – hanging from
étendu – stretching out	

Vocabulary

Le coup means 'a blow' or 'knock'. Many phrases are made up of *un coup de* . . .

un coup de pied – kick
un coup de chance – a stroke of luck
un coup de coude – a dig with the elbow, nudge
un coup de téléphone – a telephone call
un coup de vent – a gust of wind
un coup de fusil – a shot, gunshot
un coup d'oeil – a glance
un coup de main – a helping hand
un coup de foudre – love at first sight (lit.: thunderclap)
un coup de soleil – sunburn
attraper un coup de soleil – to get sunburned

AU RESTAURANT

Potages (m) – *soups*

soupe (f) à l'oignon (m) – onion soup
soupe de poisson (m) – fish soup
consommé de poulet (m) – chicken soup

Hors d'oeuvres (m)

salade (f) de betteraves (f) – beetroot salad
salade de tomates (f) – tomato salad
salade niçoise (olives (m), tomates (f), anchois (m)) – Russian salad
   (olives, tomatoes, anchovies)
crudités (m) – choice of raw vegetables
charcuterie (f) – cold meats
pâté (m) de foie (f) – liver paté
pâté maison – house paté
pamplemousse (m) – grapefruit
coquille (f) St Jacques – scallop
oeuf à la mayonnaise – egg mayonnaise
artichaut (m) – artichoke

omelette (f) au jambon – ham omelette
omelette aux champignons (m) – mushroom omelette
crevettes (f) à l'ail (m) – shrimps with garlic
moules (f) marinières – mussels cooked with wine, garlic and parsley
huîtres (f) – oysters

Plat (m) *du jour – today's main dish*

poulet rôti – roast chicken
poulet à la basquaise – chicken served in the Basque manner
canard (m) aux navets (m) – duck with turnips
canard à l'orange (f) – duck with orange
civet (m) de lapin (m) – jugged, stewed rabbit
sole meunière – sole rolled in flour and fried in butter
truite (f) de rivière (f) – river trout
agneau rôti – roast lamb
entrecôte grillée – grilled steak
côté de porc – pork (chop)
rognons (m) à la brochette – kidney kebab
chateaubriand aux pommes – thick steak with potatoes
andouillettes (f) de Bretagne – Brittany chitterling sausages

Légumes (m) – *vegetables*

haricots verts – French beans
épinards hachés – chopped spinach
pommes frites – chips, French fries
chou-fleur (m) au gratin – cauliflower in cheese sauce
carottes (f) – carrots
petits pois – peas
asperges (f) à la vinaigrette – asparagus in a vinaigrette sauce
chicorée (f) – chicory
endives braisées – braised endive
salade (f), laitue (m) – salad, lettuce

Fromages (m) – *cheeses*

chèvre (m) – goat's cheese
Camembert (m)
Pont l'Evêque (m)

Gruyère (f)
Roquefort (m)
Brie de Meaux (m)
Bleu de Bresse (m)
Carré de l'Est (m)
Neufchâtel (m)
Tomme au raisin (f)

Desserts (m) – *sweets*

fruits (m) (au choix) – choice of fruit
salade de fruits – fruit salad
tarte (f) aux pommes – apple tart
ananas (m) au kirsch – pineapple in Kirsch
glace (f) (parfum (m) au choix) – ice-cream (choice of flavours)
crêpe (f) au sucre – pancake with sugar
crêpe à la confiture – jam pancake

café (m) crème – white coffee
café filtre – black coffee
thé (m) – tea
thé au citron (m) – lemon tea

▮ LE REPAS

Le menu du jour, s'il vous plaît, Monsieur.

Voilà, Madame, Monsieur, choisissez. Vous voulez prendre un apéritif?

Un Ricard et une Suze, s'il vous plaît . . .

Alors, vous avez choisi? Qu'est-ce que je vous sers?

Nous prenons deux fois le menu à vingt-cinq. Pour ma femme, hors d'oeuvres variés, et puis le lapin. Moi je prends les moules pour commencer. Expliquez-moi ce que c'est que ces andouillettes-là.

C'est une charcuterie à base de boyaux de porc coupés en morceaux et enserrés dans une partie du gros intestin, Monsieur. C'est une spécialité de la maison. Vous ne les avez jamais essayé? C'est très bon.

J'en suis sûr. Mais je prendrai autre chose . . . une entrecôte.

Vous voulez votre steack bien cuit ou saignant?

Bien cuit.

Et qu'est-ce que je vous sers comme boisson? du vin? du cidre? de la bière?

Un quart de rouge et de l'eau minérale . . .

Voilà! Bon appétit! . . .

Un dessert? du fromage? Qu'est-ce que vous voulez comme dessert?

Du Roquefort et du chèvre. Et pour terminer, apportez-nous deux cafés filtres et deux cognacs . . .

L'addition, s'il vous plaît! Le service est-il compris ou non-compris?

Le service est toujours compris maintenant, Monsieur.

THE MEAL

The menu, please, waiter.

There you are, madam, sir, please choose. Would you like an aperitif?

One Ricard and a Suze, please . . .

Well, have you decided? What can I serve you?

We are having the menu at 25F twice. For my wife, mixed hors d'oeuvres and then the rabbit. I'm having the mussels to start with. Explain to me what these andouillettes are.

It's a meat dish based on offal cut into pieces and squeezed into a piece of the large intestine, sir. It's a speciality of the house. Haven't you ever tried it? It's very good.

I'm sure. But I'll have something else. A steak.

Would you like your steak well done or rare?

Well done.

And what can I get you to drink? wine? cider? beer?

A quarter litre of red wine and mineral water . . .

There you are. Enjoy your meal! . . .

Dessert? Cheese? What pudding would you like?

Some Roquefort and some goat's cheese. And to finish, bring us two black coffees and two brandies . . .

The bill, please. Is the service included or not included?

You have 15 per cent extra to pay, sir.

LESSON FOURTEEN

CONDITIONAL TENSE

The meaning of this tense is 'I would . . .' or 'I should . . .'
   For all verbs, add the imperfect tense endings to the future stem:

	donner	*finir*	*être*
je	donner+ais	finir+ais	ser+ais
tu	donner+ais	finir+ais	ser+ais
il	donner+ait	finir+ait	ser+ait
nous	donner+ions	finir+ions	ser+ions
vous	donner+iez	finir+iez	ser+iez
ils	donner+aient	finir+aient	ser+aient

Exercise

1. I would have. 2. He would see. 3. We should know. 4. They (m) would receive. 5. You (sing.) would like. 6. She would begin. 7. You (pl) would sell. 8. I would drink. 9. He would discover. 10. I would serve.

1. J'aurais. 2. Il verrait. 3. Nous saurions. 4. Ils recevraient. 5. Tu voudrais. 6. Elle commencerait. 7. Vous vendriez. 8. Je boirais. 9. Il découvrait. 10. Je servirais.

Remaining irregular future/conditional stems

aller (go) – j'irai(s)
acheter (buy) – j'achéterai(s)
appeler (call) – j'appellerai(s)
envoyer (send) – j'enverrai(s)
jeter (throw) – je jetterai(s)
faire (do) – je ferai(s)

courir (run) – je courrai(s)
cueillir (gather) – je cueillerai(s)
mourir (die) – je mourrai(s)
tenir (hold) – je tiendrai(s)
venir (come) – je viendrai(s)

Use of the conditional

Il m'a dit qu'il le ferait tout de suite – He told me he'd do it straight
   away

Je leur ai dit de partir quand ils seraient prêts – I told them to leave when they were ready

Il m'a promis de venir quand il aurait fini son travail – He promised me he'd come when he had (would have) finished his work

Seriez-vous Monsieur un Tel? – Would you be Mr So-and-so?

Vous n'auriez pas un stylo, par hasard? – You wouldn't have a pen, by any chance?

Même s'il me le disait, je ne le croirais pas – Even if he told (would tell) me that, I wouldn't believe him

CONDITIONAL PERFECT TENSE

j'aurais été – I would have been
il aurait mangé – he would have eaten
je serais venu – I would have come
il serait tombé – he would have fallen

FUTURE PERFECT TENSE

j'aurai eu – I will have had
il aura fait – he will have done
je serai entré – I will have gone in
elle sera partie – she will have left

PLUPERFECT TENSE

The meaning of this tense is 'I had . . .', etc.

Use the imperfect of the auxiliary with the past participle:

j'avais donné	je m'étais couché(e)
tu avais donné	tu t'étais couché(e)
il avait donné	il s'était couché
nous avions donné	nous nous étions couché(e)s
vous aviez donné	vous vous étiez couché(e)s
ils avaient donné	ils s'étaient couchés

Agreement of the past participle follows the normal rules:

Les porteurs étaient partis pour boire un coup – The porters had gone off to have a drink

Exercise

1. He will have put. 2. She would have gone in. 3. They (f) had come down. 4. I (m) had got up. 5. I (f) shall have gone. 6. I should have taken. 7. You (m sing.) had stayed. 8. We had beaten. 9. They (f) would have followed. 10. We should have refused. 11. You (pl) had talked.

1. Il aura mis. 2. Elle serait entrée. 3. Elles étaient descendues. 4. Je m'étais levé. 5. Je serai partie. 6. J'aurais mis. 7. Tu étais resté. 8. Nous avions battu. 9. Elles auraient suivi. 10. Nous aurions refusé. 11. Vous aviez parlé.

'IF' CLAUSES – SEQUENCE OF TENSES

si + present   followed by   future
si + imperfect   followed by   conditional
si + pluperfect followed by   conditional perfect

S'il fait beau, nous sortirons – If it's fine, we will go out
S'il pleuvait, j'irais au cinéma – If it were raining, I would go to the cinema
S'il avait plu, je serais allé au cinéma – If it had rained, I would have gone to the cinema

DEMONSTRATIVE PRONOUN – THE ONE, THAT, THOSE

	Masc.	*Fem.*
Sing.	celui	celle
Plural	ceux	celles

Ce n'est pas ma faute. C'est celle de Jean – It's not my fault. It's John's
Qui ça? Celui qui chante? Mais non, l'autre, celle qui danse – Who's that? The one who's singing? No, the other, the one who's dancing
Levez la main tous ceux qui sont d'accord – Put up your hands, all those who agree
Quelle voiture as-tu achetée? Celle qu j'ai vue hier – Which car did you buy? The one I saw yesterday

Celui de mon copain est meilleur que le tien – My mate's is better than yours.

Quel gâteau voulez-vous? Celui-là – Which cake do you want? That one

Quelles boîtes? Celles-ci? Non, celles-là – Which boxes? These? No, those.

RELATIVE PRONOUN – WITH PREPOSITIONS

	Masc.	*Fem.*
Sing.	lequel	laquelle
Plural	lesquels	lesquelles

Lequel is used with prepositions to mean 'with which', 'with whom', 'by which', etc.:

Les gens parmi lesquels j'habite – The people among whom I live

La falaise contre laquelle je me suis endormi – The cliff against which I fell asleep

L'argent, sans lequel on ne peut jamais réussir – Money, without which one can never succeed

When *lequel* etc. is used with *à* and *de*, the same contractions are made as with the definite article:

auquel	duquel
à laquelle	de laquelle
auxquels	desquels
auxquelles	desquelles

Le fonctionnaire auquel il s'était adressé – The official to whom he had applied (spoken)

Le magasin duquel je suis venu – The shop from which I came

Des questions auxquelles je n'avais pas de réponse – Questions to which I had no answer

However, 'in which' is more easily translated by *où*:

la maison où j'habite – the house in which I live

à l'époque où nous sommes – the times we live in

le pays où je suis né – the country in which I was born

le village d'où il venait – the village from which he came

Lequel? in questions means 'Which one?'

Laquelle voulez-vous? Celle-là? – Which one do you want? That one?

Lesquels a-t-il pris? Ceux-ci? – Which ones did he take? These?

Lequel avez-vous choisi? Celui-là? – Which one have you chosen? That one?

COUNTRIES / LANGUAGES/PEOPLE

Country	French	Language/People
Great Britain	la Grande Bretagne	britannique
England	l'Angleterre (f)	anglais(e)
Wales	le Pays de Galles	gallois(e)
Scotland	l'Écosse (f)	écossais(e)
Ireland	l'Irlande (f)	irlandais(e)
Austria	l'Autriche (f)	autrichien(-ne)
Belgium	la Belgique	belge
China	la Chine	chinois(e)
Canada	le Canada	canadien(-ne)
W. Germany	l'Allemagne (f) de l'Ouest	allemand(e)
E. Germany	l'Allemagne de l'Est	allemand(e)
Holland	la Hollande	hollandais(e)
Italy	l'Italie (f)	italien(-ne)
Japan	le Japon	japonais(e)
Portugal	le Portugal	portugais(e)
Russia	la Russie l'URSS	russe
Spain	l'Espagne	espagnol(e)
Switzerland	la Suisse	suisse
USA	les États-Unis (m)	américain(e)
Europe	l'Europe (f)	européen(-ne)

Adjectives referring to names of towns and provinces

Bordeaux – bordelais(-e)
Brest – brestois(-e)
la Bretagne – breton(-ne)
la Californie – californien(-ne)
Cannes – cannois(-e)

la Normandie – normand(e)
Paris – parisien(-ne)
Pau – palois(e)
la Provence – provençal(e)
Reims – rémois(e)

Lyon – lyonnais(e)	Toulouse – toulousain(e)
Milan – milanais(e)	Tours – tourangeau(lle)
Nantes – nantais(e)	Valence – valentinois(e)
Nice – niçois(e)	la Venise – vénitien(ne)
Nîmes – nîmois(e)	

An initial capital is used when referring to the people from a district: les Bretons – the Bretons.

■ LE CHAMPIONNAT DE FOOTBALL – NANTES TRÉBUCHE À NÎMES

C'est contre le cours du jeu que les Nîmois avaient regagné les vestiaires à la mi-temps, menés pas deux buts à un. Ils avaient attaqué la rencontre sur un rhythme particulièrement alerte et porté la preuve qu'ils pouvaient manoeuvrer avec beaucoup de spontanéïté. On avait alors le spectacle d'une offensive qui, par la vitesse de course de Duclos, les dribbles et les ouvertures précieuses de Dupont et les actions déconcertantes de Duchamp, troublait l'ordonnance d'une équipe nantaise qui donnait l'impression d'un boxeur saoulé de coups au bord du K.O. La réussite avait d'ailleurs souri sur les Méridionaux puisque, sur une action de Dupont, le rapide Duclos était intervenu avant le gardien visiteur et avait ouvert la marque.

On reconnaîtra le mérite aux Nîmois, après avoir concédé un premier but qui aurait pu les désorienter, d'avoir compté sur leur football collectif et sur leur métier pour calmer l'ardeur de leurs rivaux. La contre-attaque des Nîmois marquait le déroulement d'une deuxième mi-temps qui, malgré quelques insuffisances de la défense nantaise a, en ce début de saison, donné pleinement satisfaction à un public relativement nombreux.

FOOTBALL CHAMPIONSHIP – NANTES TRIP UP AT NIMES

It was against the run of play that Nîmes had returned to the changing-rooms at half-time, down by two goals to one. They had opened the game with a particularly brisk rhythm and proved that they could operate with lots of spontaneity. Then we had the sight of an offensive, which by the speed of the running of Dupont, the dribbling and the valuable openings of Duclos and the disconcerting moves of Duchamp, troubled the composure of a Nantes team which gave the impression of a punch-drunk boxer on the edge of a knock-out. Besides, the Southerners had been successful since, from a move by Dupont, the speedy Duclos had cut in front of the visiting goalkeeper and had opened the score.

Credit will be given to Nîmes, after having conceded a first goal which could have thrown them off-balance, for having relied on the teamwork of their football and on their craft to calm the enthusiasm of their rivals. The Nîmes counter-attack was the feature of the events of a second half which, in spite of a few deficiencies in the Nantes defence, gave, at the beginning of the season, full satisfaction to a relatively large crowd.

LESSON FIFTEEN

PASSIVE VOICE

The passive is formed quite simply with *être* + past participle. The past participle is used as an adjective and agrees with the subject:

la maison est détruite – the house is destroyed

All the tenses are made up as one would expect:

être blessé(e) – to be hurt
avoir été blessé(e) – to have been hurt
étant blessé(e) – being hurt
je suis blessé(e) – I am hurt
j'étais blessé(e) – I was hurt
je serai blessé(e) – I shall be hurt
je serais blessé(e) – I would be hurt
j'ai été blessé(e) – I have been hurt
j'avais été blessé(e) – I had been hurt
j'aurai(s) été blessé(e) – I will (would) have been hurt
soyez blessé(e) – be hurt

The French passive is less frequently used than the English. It is often avoided by the use of *on* + active verb:

On a mis le couvert – The table has been laid

On va fermer la boutique – The shop is going to be closed
On a remporté la victoire (sur) – A victory has been won (over)
On va élever les prix – Prices will be raised

Reflexive verbs may convey the passive sense:

Comment s'appelle-t-il? – What is he called? (What's his name?)
Ça ne se dit pas – That isn't said
Le théâtre s'ouvre à dix heures – The theatre is open at 10 o'clock
Je ne m'étonne pas que . . . – I'm not surprised that . . .

Only verbs which take a direct object can be made passive:

demander *à* quelqu'un de faire quelque chose
dire quelque chose *à* quelqu'un
On m'a demandé de m'en aller – I was asked to go away
permettre *à* quelqu'un de faire quelque chose
On lui permet de faire la visite – He is allowed to visit
Il m'est permis de le dire – I am allowed to say so
défendre *à* quelqu'un de faire quelque chose
On va leur demander de payer – They will be asked to pay
On lui a défendu l'alcool – He was forbidden to drink alcohol
On nous a défendu d'entrer – We were told not to come in
On lui a dit d'attendre – He was told to wait

Notice the difference between a state and an action:

state	*action*
la porte est ouverte	la porte s'ouvre
the door is open	the door is opened (opens)
les magasins sont fermés	les magasins se ferment
the shops are shut	the shops are shutting (shut)
ce livre est vendu	ce livre se vend
this book is sold	this book sells (is selling)

IMPORTER – TO MATTER

This verb is impersonal and is used only in the *il* form:

N'importe – It doesn't matter
Qu'importe? – What does it matter?
Peu m'importe s'il ne vient pas – It matters little to me (I don't care) if he doesn't come

Qu'importe si vous êtes malade? – What does it matter if you're ill?

N'importe qui pourrait gagner le gros lot – Anyone could win the jackpot

Tu dis n'importe quoi – You're talking rubbish

Ils bavardaient de n'importe quoi – They were gossiping about any old thing

aller n'importe où – to go anywhere at all

conduire n'importe comment – to drive any old how

arriver à n'importe quelle heure – to arrive at any time

Chaque means 'each', 'every', as an adjective:

Le facteur vient chaque jour – The postman comes every day

Chacun(e) means 'each' (one), 'every' (one):

chacun de mes amis – each one of my friends

chacune de ces maisons – each one of these houses

chacun pour soi – every man for himself

je donne du pain à chacun – I'm giving bread to everyone

Quelques-un(e)s means 'a few', 'some', standing apart from the noun:

Quelques-uns des spectateurs sont saôuls – Some of the spectators are drunk

Combien en voulez-vous? Quelques-unes – How many (f) do you want? Some

INDEFINITE ADJECTIVES AND PRONOUNS

Il se passe quelque chose – Something's happening

Il y a quelque chose de bizarre – There's something strange

Y a-t-il quelque chose à manger? – Is there anything to eat?

à quelque distance du bureau – at some distance from the office

au bout de quelques minutes – after a few minutes

Il y a quelqu'un dans le jardin – There's somebody in the garden

Voilà quelqu'un d'intéressant – There's somebody interesting

C'est un film très quelconque – That film's nothing special

Sont-ils quelque part à la cuisine? – Are they somewhere in the kitchen?

Sans doute ils sont autre part – No doubt they're somewhere else
Ça ne vaut pas grand'chose – That's not worth a lot
Il n'y a pas grand'chose ce soir – There isn't much on this evening
à peu de chose près – more or less
Il a tout fait avec peu de chose – He's done everything with little
Alors ça, c'est autre chose – Well, that's something else
Il n'y a aucun problème – There's no problem
Aucune élève n'a été reçue à cet examen – No pupil (f) has passed
   this exam

   Tel, *telle*, *tels*, *telles* mean 'such':

avec une telle voiture – with such a car
de telles personnes – such people
plusieurs groupes, tels que les mineurs – several groups, such as
   the miners

   Tel cannot qualify another adjective. Instead, *si* or *tellement* is
used:

une si belle journée – such a fine day
des gens tellement agressifs – such aggressive people

Exercise

1. The ticket office shuts at six. 2. The bill was paid. 3. We (m)
would have been insured. 4. You (sing.) were given a ticket. 5. He
behaved carelessly (anyhow). 6. Each one is 2 metres thick. 7. I
know somebody in Tours. 8. I don't know much. 9. A few of my
friends (m). 10. You (sing.) will have no difficulty in finding the way.
11. The roads are so busy. 12. Such dangerous ideas.

1. Le guichet se ferme à six heures. 2. L'addition a été payée. 3. Nous
aurions été assurés. 4. On t'a donné un billet. 5. Il se comportait
n'importe comment. 6. Chacun a une épaisseur de deux mètres. 7.
Je connais quelqu'un à Tours. 8. Je ne sais pas grand'chose. 9.
Quelques-uns de mes amis. 10. Tu n'auras aucune difficulté à
trouver le chemin. 11. Les routes sont tellement encombrées. 12.
Des idées tellement dangereuscs.

DEPUIS (since) + TENSES

English   *French*
have been   =   (a) present
had been   =   (b) imperfect

(a) Depuis quand étes-vous là? – How long (since when) have
     you been there?

   J'habite ici depuis trois ans – I've been living here for (since)
     three years

   Je vous attends depuis hier – I've been waiting for you since
     yesterday

(b) Depuis quand attendiez-vous? – (since) How long had you
     been waiting?

   Il était absent depuis quinze jours – he had been away (since)
     a fortnight

   Voilà is used in much the same way:

· Voilà trois mois que je ne suis pas en France – I haven't been in
   France for three months

DEFINITE ARTICLE + PARTS OF THE BODY

When parts of the body are not the subject of the sentence, the
possessive adjective is replaced by the definite article:

Il a levé la main – He raised his hand
Elle a les yeux bleus – She has blue eyes

   When necessary, the owner is specified by the indirect object
pronoun:

Je lui ai pris la main – I took his (her) hand
On lui bande les yeux – They blindfold his (her) eyes
Il se lave les pieds – He's washing his feet

■ CHEZ LE COIFFEUR – AT THE HAIRDRESSER

Vocabulary

la barbe – beard	le shampooing – shampoo, wash
le favori – sideburn	la teinture – tint, dye
la frange – fringe	couper – to cut
le front – forehead	dégager – to free
la (les) moustache(s) – moustache	friser – to curl
	rafraîchir -- to trim
les pellicules (f) – dandruff	raser – to shave
la permanente – perm	tailler – to cut, shape
la raie – parting	

Messieurs

Comment voulez-vous que je vous coupe les cheveux? Vous voulez le front bien dégagé?

Je les voudrais ni trop longs, ni trop courts. Mais surtout pas taillés en brosse.

Eh bien, je vais vous rafraîchir un peu les cheveux. Vous portez la raie à gauche ou au milieu? Est-ce que je vous rase la barbe?

Laissez la barbe, la moustache et les favoris.

Vous voulez un shampooing?

Merci non, mais coupez les cheveux à mes deux gosses-là.

Dames

Faites-moi une permanente, s'il vous plaît. Mais je ne veux pas les cheveux trop frisés. Pas de teinture.

Prenez-vous un shampooing contre les cheveux gras ou secs?

Ça m'est égal, j'ai des cheveux normaux. Mais mettez quelque chose contre les pellicules. Coupez les cheveux plus ou moins courts sur les deux côtés, avec une frange couvrant le front. Et par derrière légèrement longs.

Gentlemen

How would you like me to cut your hair? Do you want your forehead well uncovered?

I'd like it neither too long nor too short. But especially not a crew cut.

Well, I'll give you a slight trim. Do you have your parting on the left or in the middle? Shall I shave your beard?

Leave the beard, the moustache and the sideburns.

Do you want your hair washed?

No thanks, but cut my two kids' hair.

Ladies

Give me a perm, please. But I don't want my hair too curly. No tinting.

Would you like a shampoo for greasy or dry hair?

I don't mind, I have normal hair. But use a medicated (anti-dandruff) shampoo. Cut my hair more or less short at the sides, with a fringe covering the forehead. And slightly long at the back.

■ CHEZ LE MÉDECIN – AT THE DOCTOR

Vocabulary

le comprimé – tablet	une ordonnance – prescription
la consultation – appointment	le toux – cough
la douleur – pain	le traitement – treatment
une entorse – twisted ankle	respirer – to breathe
la grippe – flu	souffrir – to be in pain

Pouvez-vous me prendre cet après-midi?

Ça va être très difficile. J'ai des consultations jusqu'à sept heures.

Mais je souffre beaucoup. J'ai une rage de dents, une migraine, et puis je me suis cassé la jambe hier; j'ai attrapé la grippe, j'ai des douleurs au ventre, je respire avec difficulté, j'ai une toux affreuse, je me suis donné une entorse et j'ai une allergie aux pollens. Quel traitement prescrivez-vous?

Prenez deux comprimés d'aspirine trois fois par jour. Renoncez à fumer tout de suite. Ne buvez pas d'alcool. Prenez régulièrement de l'exercice. Venez me revoir la semaine prochaine. Mes heures de consultation sont de six à dix heures tous les soirs.

Can you fit me in this afternoon?

That'll be very difficult. I have appointments until 7 o'clock.

But I'm in great pain. I have toothache, a migraine, and then I broke my leg yesterday; I've caught flu, I've got pains in my stomach, I'm having difficulty breathing, I've got a terrible cough, I twisted my ankle and I have hay-fever. What treatment do you prescribe?

Take two aspirin tablets three times a day. Give up smoking immediately. Don't drink any alcohol. Take exercise regularly. Come and see me again next week. My surgery hours are from 6 to 10 every evening.

LESSON SIXTEEN

SUBJUNCTIVE

Present subjunctive

The subjunctive stem for regular verbs is taken from the 3rd person plural present indicative tense:

donner	-ils donnent – je donn+e
finir	-ils finissent – je finiss+e
vendre	-ils vendent – je vend+e

The endings are *-e, -es, -e, -ions, -iez, -ent*:

que je	donne	finisse	vende
que tu	donnes	finisses	vendes
qu' il	donne	finisse	vende
que nous	donnions	finissions	vendions
que vous	donniez	finissiez	vendiez
qu' ils	donnent	finissent	vendent

A few verbs have irregular subjunctive stems, but use the same endings:

faire — que je *fasse*, nous *fassions*, ils *fassent*

aller   – que j'*aille*, nous allions, vous alliez, ils *aillent*
savoir   – que je *sache*, nous *sachions*, ils *sachent*
pouvoir – que je *puisse*, nous *puissions*, ils *puissent*
vouloir – que je *veuille*, nous voulions, vous vouliez, ils *veuillent*
venir   – que je *vienne*, nous venions, vous veniez, ils *viennent*

Avoir and *être* are irregular:

	avoir	*être*
je (j')	aie	sois
tu	aies	sois
il	ait	soit
nous	ayons	soyons
vous	ayez	soyez
ils	aient	soient

For other common irregular subjunctive forms, consult the index of irregular verbs.

The perfect subjunctive is formed with the present subjunctive of the auxiliary verb and the past participle:

il est venu – avant qu'il soit venu . . .
nous avons appris – jusqu'à ce que nous ayons appris . . .

Exercise: put the following into the present subjunctive:

1. Il conduit. 2. Nous mentons. 3. Tu lis. 4. Elle craint. 5. Vous mettez. 6. Je prends. 7. Nous suivons. 8. Ils reçoivent. 9. Je tiens. 10. Tu meurs.

1. Il conduise. 2. Nous mentions. 3. Tu lises. 4. Elle craigne. 5. Vous mettiez. 6. Je prenne. 7. Nous suivions. 8. Ils reçoivent. 9. Je tienne. 10. Tu meures.

Use of the subjunctive

The subjunctive is often described as the mood of doubt and possibility. In English we say:

I *am* learning French – *indicative*
If I *were* you, I would learn French – *subjunctive*

If I *were* to score now, nothing could stop us – *subjunctive*

1 As a main verb, the subjunctive is rarely used, except in certain set expressions, or in the 3rd person as an imperative:

Vive la France! – Long live France!
Autant que je sache – As far as I know
Qu'il fasse ce qu'il veut! – Let him do what he wants!
Qu'il prenne un emploie! – Let him get a job!

2 The subjunctive is obligatory after certain conjunctions:

*Bien qu'*il soit marié, il aime beaucoup les filles – Although he's married, he likes girls a lot

*Quoiqu'*il y ait plusieurs cinémas en ville, moi je n'y vais jamais – Although there are several cinemas in town, I never go

Jusqu'à ce que tu t'en ailles, je vais rester ici – Until you go, I will stay here

*Pourvu qu'*il fasse ses devoirs, il peut sortir ce soir – Provided that he does his homework, he can go out this evening

*Avant qu'*il se soit levé le matin, sa femme a déjà quitté la maison – Before he has got up in the morning, his wife has already left the house

Je vous apporterai le carte, *afin que* vous puissiez choisir – I will bring you the menu, so that you can choose

Ils montent l'escalier, *sans qu'*on les voie – They climb the stairs without anyone seeing them

À moins que requires the subjunctive and *ne*:

Il va venir, *à moins qu'*il *ne* soit malade – He will come, unless he is ill

Avant de (+ infinitive) is used rather than *avant que* (+ subjunctive) when the subject of both clauses is the same:

Avant de se rendre à l'aéroport, il a acheté des cadeaux – Before going to the airport, he bought some presents

3 The subjunctive is used in clauses dependent on verbs of emotion, such as:

vouloir que – to wish that   s'étonner que – to be surprised that
désirer que – to wish that   c'est dommage que – it's a pity that

regretter que – to be sorry that

quelle chance que – what luck that

être content que – to be happy that

avoir peur que (+ ne) – to be afraid that

Je regrette que vous n'ayez pu venir – I'm sorry you couldn't come

Quelle chance que nous nous soyons rencontrés – What luck that we met

C'est dommage que vous n'ayez pas d'argent – It's a pity you haven't any money

Nous voulons que vous veniez avec nous – We want you to come with us

J'ai peur qu'ils ne viennent pas – I'm afraid they're not coming

4 The subjunctive is used after expressions of possibility and doubt:

Il est possible que vous ayez raison – It's possible that you're right

Il se peut que vous vous trompiez – It could be that you're wrong

Je ne crois pas qu'il soit mort – I don't think he's dead

5 The subjunctive is used after expressions of command:

Ils exigent que nous payions tout de suite – They insist that we pay at once

Permettez que je vous serve – Allow me to serve you

6 The subjunctive is used in clauses depending on a superlative, or on *seul*, *premier* and *dernier*:

C'est le meilleur spectacle que je n'aie jamais vue – It's the best show that I've ever seen

C'est le seul moyen qu'on ait trouvé de traiter cette maladie – It's the only way they've found of treating this illness

7 The subjunctive is used after *il faut que*, *qu'importe que* and *je ne crois pas que*:

Il faut que vous alliez à la gare – You have to go to the station

Qu'importe que vous soyez pauvre! – What does it matter if you're poor!

Je ne crois pas qu'il soit parti – I don't think he has left

8 The subjunctive is used after the following concessive expressions:

quel(lle) que – whoever, whatever (adjective)
quoi que – whatever (pronoun)
quelque . . . que – whatever, however (adjective)
si . . . que – however (adverb)
où que – wherever (adverb)
qui que – whoever

quel que soit votre avis . . . whatever your opinion may be . . .
quelle que soit la distance . . . whatever the distance may be . . .
quoi que ce soit . . . – whatever it may be . . .
quelques ennuyants qu'ils soient . . . – however boring they may be . . .
si fatigué que vous soyez . . . – however tired you are . . .
où que vous alliez . . . – wherever you go . . .
qui que vous soyez . . . – whoever you are . . .

VERB CONSTRUCTIONS WITH THE INFINITIVE

au coucher, au lever du soleil – at sunset, sunrise
entrez sans frapper – come in without knocking
Tu agis sans réfléchir – You act without thinking
Avant de sortir, fermez la porte à clef – Before going out, lock the door
Il faut gagner au lieu de perdre – You must win instead of losing
Prenez ce briquet pour allumer votre cigare – Take this lighter to light your cigar
après avoir fait la vaisselle – after having washed up
Comment trouver la solution? – How do we find the answer?
être en train de faire quelque chose – to be (in the process of) doing something
Tu sais *jouer aux* échecs? – Can you play chess?
Je l'entends *jouer du* piano – I can hear him playing the piano
Je t'invite à boire un coup – I'll buy you a drink
Il s'intéresse à lire – He's interested in reading
Ça m'empêche de sortir – That stops me going out
Je regrette de t'avoir dérangé – I'm sorry to have disturbed you

SHOPPING (See also pp. 32–3)

Shops	People
une épicerie – grocer's	un épicier – grocer
la boucherie – butcher's	un boucher – butcher
la boulangerie – baker's	un boulanger – baker
la pâtisserie – cake-shop	un pâtissier – pastrycook
la bijouterie – jeweller's	un bijoutier – jeweller
la confiserie – sweet-shop	un confisier – sweet-seller
la quincaillerie – ironmonger's	un quincaillier – ironmonger
la pharmacie – chemist's	un pharmacien – chemist
la librairie – bookshop	un libraire – bookseller
la charcuterie – delicatessen	un charcutier – pork butcher
le magasin de chaussures – shoe-shop	un cordonnier – cobbler
le tabac – tobacconist's	un tailleur – tailor

LA GRANDE VILLE – THE BIG TOWN

Vocabulary

une ville industrielle, commerçante – an industrial, commercial town

les faubourgs, la banlieue – the outskirts, suburbs

un quartier résidentiel – a residential area

l'agglomération parisienne – the Parisian conurbation

la cité universitaire – the university halls of residence

la capitale financière – the financial capital

les transports urbains – public (city) transport

la grand'place – the main square

le rond-point – roundabout

un immeuble de six étages – a six-storey building

habiter un appartement dans un immeuble – to live in a block of flats

la gare routière – bus station

un panneau-réclame – advertisement hoarding, billboard

les grands centres charbonniers – the big coal-mining areas

un stationnement pour taxis – taxi rank

faire le va et vient entre – to commute between

le boulevard périphérique – ring road
le passage souterrain – subway
une perspective sur la tour Eiffel – a view of the Eiffel Tower
la rive gauche, droite – left, right bank
la cité de Carcassonne – the old city of Carcassonne
un jardin public – a park

■ Translation

J'habite un village de montagne, à peu de distance de Bionnas, ville industrielle, le principal centre français de production d'objets en matière plastique, dans les monts du Jura, à moins d'une heure de voiture de la frontière suisse. J'y descends souvent à la fin de l'après-midi. J'aime l'animation des villes ouvrières, à l'heure de la sortie des ateliers, les motos qui se fraient bruyamment leur chemin parmi les cyclistes, les boutiques pleines de femmes, l'odeur d'anis à la terrasse des cafés. La veille du circuit 1954, vers sept heures du soir, je descendais l'avenue Jean-Jaurès, qui est la principale artère de Bionnas. Cordélia, ma femme, m'accompagnait. Nous venions de nous arrêter devant une boutique où de violents éclairages faisait scintiller des bijoux bon marché . . . (et puis nous avons aperçu) Marie-Jeanne Lemercier qui s'avançait d'un pas tranquille au milieu des passants pressés. (Roger Vailland)

I live in a mountain village not far from Bionnas, an industrial town, the main centre in France for the production of plastic products, in the Jura mountains, less than half an hour's drive from the Swiss border. I often go down there in the late afternoon. I like the busy atmosphere of working-class towns at the time of the exodus from the workshops, the motorbikes noisily forcing their way through the cyclists, the shops full of women, the smell of aniseed on the café terraces. The day before the 1954 race, about 7 o'clock in the evening, I was going down Avenue Jean-Jaurès, the main thorough-fare of Bionnas. Cordelia, my wife, was with me. We had just stopped in front of a shop in which brilliant lighting made the cheap jewellery sparkle . . . (and then we spotted) Marie-Jeanne Lemercier walking quietly through the throng of passers-by.

LESSON SEVENTEEN

PAST HISTORIC TENSE

In the spoken language, the past historic tense is never used. But in written French, it is the most widely-used tense. It is the narrative tense corresponding to the perfect tense in speech. It describes completed actions which took place at some time in the past (I gave, I finished, I drank), but conveys no idea of duration of time. Duration of time past is always expressed by the imperfect.

The past historic is always formed one of three ways. They are:

	donner	*finir*	*boire*
je	donn + ai	fin + is	bus
tu	donn + as	fin + is	bus
il	donn + a	fin + it	but
nous	donn + âmes	fin + îmes	bûmes
vous	donn + âtes	fin + îtes	bûtes
ils	donn + èrent	fin + irent	burent

All *-er* verbs follow *donner*, all regular *-ir* and *-re* verbs follow *finir*, and some irregular verbs follow *boire*. Here is a list of other common past historic forms:

like finir	*like boire*
s'asseoir – je m'assis	être – je fus
cueillir – je cueillis	avoir – j'eus
dormir – je dormis	mourir – je mourus
fuir – je fuis	apercevoir – j'aperçus
offrir – j'offris	devoir – je dus
ouvrir – j'ouvris	pouvoir – je pus
partir – je partis	recevoir – je reçus
voir – je vis	savoir – je sus
battre – je battis	vouloir – je voulus
conduire – je conduisis	il faut – il fallut
craindre – je craignis	il pleut – il plut
dire – je dis	connaître – je connus
écrire – j'écrivis	courir – je courus
faire – je fis	croire – je crus

mettre – je mis
prendre – je pris

lire – je lus
vivre – je vécus

There are only two total exceptions:

	venir	*tenir*
je	vins	tins
tu	vins	tins
il	vint	tint
nous	vînmes	tînmes
vous	vîntes	tîntes
ils	vinrent	tinrent

Exercise: change into the past historic:

1. Je suis allé. 2. Il est sorti. 3. Tu as répondu. 4. Nous nous sommes
levés. 5. J'ai vu. 6. Ils ont pu. 7. Vous avez tenu. 8. Je suis descendu.
9. Elle est tombée. 10. Vous avez mangé.

1. J'allai. 2. Il sortit. 3. Tu répondis. 4. Nous nous levâmes. 5. Je vis.
6. Ils purent. 7. Vous tîntes. 8. Je descendis. 9. Elle tomba. 10. Vous
mangeâtes.

PAST ANTERIOR TENSE

'When he had done this, he did that':

spoken:	pluperfect	perfect
written:	past anterior	past historic

The past anterior tense is formed by combining the past historic of
the auxiliary verb with a past participle: *J'eus fait* – I had done. It
replaces the pluperfect in time clauses where the main verb is in the
past historic. It is thus a written tense, not used in speech. So to
translate 'When he had done this, he did that' into *written* French,
the past anterior tense would be used, followed by the past historic,
while in the *spoken* language the pluperfect is used, followed by the
perfect tense.

The spoken and written languages contrasted

Quand (lorsqu') il avait fini le repas, il a fumé une cigarette

Quand (lorsqu') il eut fini le repas, il fuma une cigarette
When he had finished the meal, he smoked a cigarette

Dès qu'ils étaient partis, nous nous sommes couchés
Dés qu'ils furent partis, nous nous couchâmes
As soon as they had left, we went to bed

À peine étais-je arrivé à Londres, qu'il s'est mis à neiger
À peine fus-je à Londres, qu'il se mit à neiger
Hardly had I arrived in London, when it began to snow

Aussitôt qu'il avait chanté, nous nous sommes endormis
Aussitôt qu'il eut chanté, nous nous endormîmes
As soon as he had sung, we fell asleep

(Note that *aussitôt que* takes the indicative and is never followed by the subjunctive.)

The past historic and the perfect tenses are contrasted in the following passage.

■ DES BANDITS TIRENT POUR COUVRIR LEUR FUITE DANS LE NEUVIÈME ARRONDISSEMENT

Dans le bureau de change, 59 Avenue des États-Unis, les deux clients attendaient patiemment qu'on s'occupe d'eux. Ils avaient une trentaine d'années, étaient bien vêtus, polis. Or, leur tour venu, ce ne fut pas des travellers-cheques qu'ils sortirent de leur poches, mais deux pistolets qu'ils mirent sous le nez du gérant.

'Ouvrez le tiroir-caisse et le coffre,' lui enjoignirent-ils.

En quelques minutes, ils raflèrent environ 10,000 francs en billets et s'enfuirent à bord d'une Renault jaune.

'Pendant que ma femme téléphonait à la police, j'ai sauté dans ma voiture et je les ai retrouvés à un feu rouge, place de l'Opéra. J'ai appelé un agent qui est monté dans sa voiture, et la poursuite a repris. La Renault s'est garée rue Scribe. Les trois hommes sont descendus et se sont séparés. L'un d'entre eux s'est dirigé vers le boulevard des Capucines et a été arrêté aussitôt.'

Les deux autres gangsters se heurtèrent de leur côté, à hauteur du square Louis-Jouvet, à des agents venus en renfort. Ils n'hésitèrent pas à ouvrir le feu pour couvrir leur fuite. Un passant fut légèrement blessé au cuir chevelu. Les deux hommes ne furent pas rattrapés.

ROBBERS OPEN FIRE TO COVER THEIR ESCAPE IN THE 9TH ARRONDISSEMENT

In the exchange bureau, 59 Avenue des Etats-Unis, the two customers were waiting patiently to be served. They were about 30, well dressed, polite. Well, when their turn came it wasn't travellers' cheques that they took out of their pockets, but two guns which they shoved under the manager's nose.

'Open the cash drawer and the safe,' they told him.

In a few minutes, they carried off about 10,000 francs in notes and made their getaway in a yellow Renault.

'While my wife was calling the police, I jumped into my car and caught up with them at the traffic lights on the place de l'Opéra. I called a policeman who got into his car and the chase was on again. The Renault parked in the rue Scribe. The three men got out and separated. One of them made for the boulevard des Capucines and was arrested straight away.'

The two other robbers for their part ran into police reinforcements up in Louis Jouvet Square. They did not hesitate to open fire to cover their escape. A passer-by suffered a slight scalp wound. The two men were not apprehended.

LESSON EIGHTEEN

LETTERS

French letter-writing is conducted with what might seem to us to be almost Victorian politeness and formality. Etiquette must be respected.

Formules de politesse

The following are all ways of writing 'Yours faithfully':

Veuillez agréer, Monsieur, mes salutations distinguées.
Veuillez agréer, Madame, l'expression de mes meilleurs sentiments.

Veuillez agréer, Monsieur, l'expression de mes sentiments les
   meilleurs.
Veuillez croire, Monsieur, à l'expression de mes sentiments
   distingués.

Model letters

le 3 avril 1980

Monsieur,

   Votre dossier de candidature à un poste d'assistant français à
l'étranger est bien parvenu à l'Office National des Universités.

   J'ai le regret de vous informer qu'après examen, et en raison de
l'important excédent de candidatures pour le placement aux États-
Unis et au Canada par rapport au nombre des postes offerts dans ces
deux pays, il n'a pas été possible de donner suite à votre demande.

   Veuillez me faire savoir si, le cas échéant, je peux réorienter votre
dossier vers la Grande Bretagne.

   Recevez l'assurance de mes sentiments distingués.

Le Conseiller

3 April 1980

Dear Sir,

   Your application for a post of French assistant abroad has been
received by the National Office for Universities.

   I regret to inform you that after due consideration, and because of
the large surplus of applications for places in the United States and
Canada compared with the number of posts available in those two
countries, it has not been possible to meet your request.

   Kindly let me know if, should the occasion arise, I can re-direct
your application forms to Great Britain.

   Yours faithfully,

Counsellor

le 10 juin 1980

Monsieur,

   Nous avons l'honneur de vous rappeler l'accident survenu le 11
mars 1979 à Valence à l'assuré Jean-Pierre Duclos, employé au
service de . . .

   La responsabilité de cet accident semblant vous incomber, nous

vous informons que nous vous réclamerons, dès que nous le connaîtrons, le montant des débours de notre Caisse consécutifs à cet
accident (indemnités versées à ce jour: 450F).

Nous vous prions de prendre note que nous mettons opposition,
jusqu'à nouvel ordre, à tout règlement que vous auriez l'intention
de faire directement avec la victime ou ses ayants-droit.

Vous voudrez bien nous faire connaître vos intentions et nous
indiquer si vous êtes assuré contre les accidents et à quelle Compagnie d'Assurances. Le cas échéant, veuillez transmettre la présente
lettre à votre Compagnie d'Assurances en la priant de nous faire
connaître ses intentions.

Nous vous prions d'agréer, M., l'assurance de nos sentiments
distingués.

L'Agent du Contentieux

                                                        10 June 1980
Dear Sir,
We remind you of the accident that occurred on 11 March 1979 at
Valence to the insured Jean-Pierre Duclos, employed by . . .

As the responsibility for this accident appears to devolve upon
you, we would inform you that we are claiming from you, as soon as
we know it, the amount of payments made by us as a result of the
accident (expenses paid to the present: 450F).

Would you please take note that we oppose, until further notice,
any compromise that you may have the intention of making with the
victim or those claiming through him.

Would you please let us know of your intentions and inform us if
you are insured against accidents, and with which insurance company. If you are so insured (lit. in that case) please send this letter to
your insurance company asking it to let us know its intentions.

Yours faithfully,
Office of the Legal Department

                                                   le 8 decembre 1976
Miss Joan Smith
12 High Street
Oldplace
Somerset

Mademoiselle,

Je vous remercie de votre réponse à notre annonce. Je serais heureux de savoir si vous pouviez venir pour une entrevue à notre bureau à Paris le 20 décembre à 1400 h.

Le prix de votre voyage en avion et de votre logement pour une nuit dans un hotel vous sera remboursé.

Veuillez nous faire savoir par retour du courrier si vous viendrez.

Je vous prie d'agréer, Mademoiselle, l'expression de mes salutations distinguées.

Claude Duchamp

8 December 1976

Dear Miss Smith,

Thank you for your reply to our advertisement. I would be pleased to know if you could come for an interview at our Paris office on 20 December at 2.00 pm.

The cost of your plane journey and of your accommodation for one night in a hotel will be reimbursed.

Kindly let us know by return of post if you are able to come.

Yours faithfully,

Claude Duchamp

Dimanche 16 mai

Chère Madame Leblanc,

Pardonnez-moi si je ne vous ai pas écrit plus tôt. Après le congrès nous sommes descendus tout de suite sur la Loire; nous avons visité Orléans, Blois et Tours et nous nous sommes arrêtés quelques jours à Angers, Puis, nous sommes remontés à Cherbourg, en passant par Caen et Bayeux. Enfin, ce n'était qu'hier que nous avons regagné chez nous et qu'aujourd'hui que je suis en mesure de vous écrire.

Je ne sais comment vous remercier de votre aimable hospitalité. Vous savez déjà combien nous avons joui de Paris, malgré la brièveté de notre séjour – ses monuments, ses églises, ses musées – mais ce qui nous a surtout ravi c'était d'avoir passé une soirée si agréable chez vous. Peter m'avait souvent parlé de vous et de votre famille et je suis enchantée d'avoir enfin fait votre connaissance, celle d'Henri et de vos enfants charmants, Dominique et Jean-Marc (déjà ils parlent si bien anglais – vous devez en être fière!).

Vous m'avez dit qu'à cause de votre travail vous le trouverez très difficile de quitter Paris l'été, mais si, comme prévu, Henri doit visiter Cambridge en voyage d'affaires en juillet et si vous pensez que les enfants vont s'intéresser à passer quelques jours en Angleterre, nous serions très contents de les loger tous les trois chez nous aussi longtemps qu'ils voudraient.

Comme je l'ai expliqué, nous habitons en plein centre de la ville, qui se trouve à une heure en voiture de Londres. Roger et Susan ont à peu près les mêmes âges que Jean-Marc et Dominique et ils trouveraient, j'en suis sûre, beaucoup de choses à faire ensemble. Pour les vôtres ce serait une occasion de se perfectionner en anglais et, quoique la cuisine anglaise ne soit pas l'égale de votre cuisine française, je ferais de mon mieux!

Si vous pensez que les enfants s'intéresseraient à ce projet, dites-le-moi aussitôt que possible et nous pouvons faire les préparatifs pour leur visite. En tout cas, une fois de plus je vous remercie vivement de votre hospitalité à Paris; recevez, Madame, l'expression de mes sentiments les meilleurs.

Caroline Harrison

Sunday 16 May

Dear Mrs Leblanc,

I apologise for not having written earlier. After the conference we went straight down to the Loire; we visited Orleans, Blois and Tours and we stopped for a few days in Angers. Then we went back up to Cherbourg, passing through Caen and Bayeux. Finally, it wasn't until yesterday that we arrived home and until today that I am able to write to you.

I don't know how to thank you for your kind hospitality. You already know how much we enjoyed Paris, in spite of the shortness of our visit – its sights, its churches, its museums – but what pleased us most of all was having spent such a delightful evening at your home. Peter has often talked about you and your family and I am very pleased to have met you, Henri and your lovely children, Dominique and Jean-Marc (they speak such good English already – you must be proud of them!).

You said that because of your work you will find it very difficult to leave Paris in the summer but if, as expected, Henri has to make a business trip to Cambridge in July and if you think that the children will be interested in spending a few days in England, we should be very happy for all three of them to stay with us for as long as they would like.

As I explained, we live right in the centre of the town, which is an hour's drive from London. Roger and Susan are about the same age as Jean-Marc and Dominique and they would find, I'm sure, plenty of things to do together. For yours it would be an opportunity to improve their English and, although English cooking is not the equal of your French cooking, I would do my best!

If you think that the children would be interested in this idea, let me know as soon as possible and we can make arrangements for their visit. Anyway, thank you again for your hospitality in Paris.

Yours sincerely,
Caroline Harrison

LESSON NINETEEN

L'ARGOT

There has always been a wide gap between 'official' written French and the language spoken by Frenchmen in everyday situations. To translate *l'argot* as 'slang' is in many ways misleading. *L'argot* is a vast fund of words and expressions drawn from different sources – city slang, regional dialect, cult vocabulary. A knowledge of it is essential to a good grasp of the language, yet its use is fraught with problems.

One difficulty in speaking colloquial French is to identify and use the linguistic register appropriate to any given set of circumstances. To talk to a lorry-driver in Sunday School French is as inappropriate as to address one's mother-in-law as though she were a navvy.

A second difficulty lies in recognising the degree of vulgarity of the slang expressions you use. Here, a dictionary or a textbook can provide only very general guidance. Experience is the only reliable guide.

The following pages introduce some of the slang expressions and constructions you will most commonly meet. Handle them all with care. Those marked * should be treated with caution; those marked ** with *extreme* caution.

Two alternative verbs

	foutre	*ficher*
je	fous	fiche
tu	fous	fiches
il	fout	fiche
nous	foutons	fichons
vous	foutez	fichez
ils	foutent	fichent

imperfect: je foutais   je fichais
future: je vais foutre   je vais ficher
perfect: j'ai foutu   j'ai fichu
pres. subj.: que je foute   que je fiche

Both *foutre* and *ficher* are colloquial alternatives to *faire* (to do) and *mettre* (to put). They are also used in a wide variety of other senses, often in the reflexive form:

Je m'en fous – I don't care
Il s'en fout de la politique – He doesn't give a damn about politics
Vous vous foutez de moi! – You're having me on!
foutre le bazar partout – to raise hell everywhere
Qu'est-ce que ça peut me foutre? – What does that matter to me?
foutre quelqu'un à la porte – to sling someone out
**foutre le camp – to clear off
**Va te faire foutre! – Get stuffed!
Je n'ai rien fichu aujourd'hui – I haven't done a stroke today
*fiche-moi la paix! – leave me alone!
Je m'en fiche – I don't care

Word-building

bouffer – to eat; la bouffe – grub, nosh; la bouffetance – grub, nosh
rigoler – to laugh; rigolo – funny; la rigolade – joke

bête – silly; une bêtise – blunder, (pl) nonsense; embêtant –
    irritating, a pain; embêter – to irritate, annoy
se balader – to go for a trip, a walk; la balade – trip, walk
la gueule – mouth (animal), gob, face, expression; engueuler – to
    go on at someone; une engueulade – an earful, a talking to;
    dégueulasse – disgusting; dégueuler – to vomit
en avoir marre – to be fed up with; se marrer – to enjoy oneself;
    marrant – funny, amusing

Examples

On n'a rien à bouffer – There's nothing to eat
On bouffe toujours bien chez Henri – You always get a good nosh
    at Henry's
J'aime pas la bouffetance ici – I don't like the grub here
Il n'y a pas de quoi rigoler! – That's not funny!
Faut pas rigoler avec ça – You can't play about with that
Tu rigoles! – You're joking!
Tiens, c'est rigolo, ça – Hey, that's funny
C'est de la rigolade – It's a real joke
On a huit jours pour se balader – We've got a free week
faire une balade a l'étranger – to go for a trip abroad
*Ta gueule! – Shut up!
 avoir la gueule de bois – to have a hangover
*Je vais te casser la gueule – I'm going to knock your teeth in
 Il va se casser la gueule – He's going to come a cropper
 Il est fort en gueule – He's got too much to say for himself
 Je me suis payé une belle engueulade – I really got it in the neck
    (good talking to)
 Il m'engueulait en allemand – He was going on at me in German
*C'etait vraiment dégueulasse – It was really disgusting
 faire, dire des bêtises – to make blunders, talk rubbish
 Oh, qu'il est embêtant, celui-là! – What a nuisance he is!
 Ça m'embête d'être toujours le dernier – I'm fed up with always
    being last
 J'en ai marre de tes histoires – I'm fed up with your stories
 On s'est bien marré – We had a really good time
 Il n'est pas marrant, ton copain – Your mate's not much fun

Verb usage

On se casse? On se barre? – Shall we go (split)?

On m'a dit que ma femme s'est barrée – Someone told me my wife's
  left (me)

Je te paye un verre – I'll buy you a drink

se payer la tête de quelqu'un – to make fun of someone

On va louper le train – We're going to miss the train

Faut pas louper ton tour – Mustn't miss your go

L'acteur a raté son entrée – The actor made a mess of his entrance

Il n'en rate pas une – He's always putting his foot in it

Le pneu de sa voiture a crevé – His car tyre blew out

je vais crever de faim – I'm going to starve

Je suis complètement crevé – I'm wiped out (knackered)

C'est un boulot vraiment crevant – It's a knackering job

T'as pigé? – Do you get it? (Do you understand?)

Ils n'y ont rien pigé – They haven't understood it at all

J'ai paumé le fric – I've lost the money

Il s'est paumé en route – He got lost on the way

flanquer des oeuvres d'art dans la flotte – To sling works of art into
  the river

Quelqu'un a chipé mes godasses – Someone's nicked my shoes

bosser dans une usine – to slave in a factory

File-moi cents balles! – Give us a franc!

filer à toute berzingue – to go like a bat out of hell

Abbreviations

un apéro – aperitif

une photo – photograph

un pharmaco – chemist

un mécano – mechanic

le super – high octane petrol

la fac – university

le bac – baccalaureat

extra – fantastic

sensass – wonderful

sympa – nice, pleasant

Impolite word-building

The French swear much more creatively than the English. Here are
some expressions which are in very common use and which, in spite
of appearances, are less offensive than their English translations.

*Tu viens, oui ou merde? – Are you coming or not?

*On s'emmerde ici. On s'en va? – It's boring here. Shall we go?

*un petit emmerdeur (-se) – a pain in the neck

*On a toujours des emmerdements avec eux – You always have hassles with them

*Ça doit être emmerdant – That must be a real pain

*On va sûrement se démerder – We'll certainly get by (muddle through)

**Oh, vraiment, tu me fais chier – You really get up my nose

**C'est chiant – It's a real drag

LESSON TWENTY

VERB REFERENCE TABLE

Infinitive	Imperative	Present indicative	Imperfect / Pres. p.	Future / Conditional	Perfect / Past historic	Present subjunctive
donner to give	donne donnons donnez	donne, -es, -e, donnons, -ez, -ent	donnais donnant	donnerai donnerais	avoir donné donnai	que je donne
finir to finish	finis finissons finissez	finis, -is, -it, finissons, -ez, -ent	finissais finissant	finirai finirais	avoir fini finis	que je finisse
vendre to sell	vends vendons vendez	vends, -s, vend, vendons, -ez, -ent	vendais vendant	vendrai vendrais	avoir vendu vendis	que je vende
avoir to have	aie ayons ayez	ai, as, a, avons, avez, ont	avais ayant	aurai aurais	avoir eu eus	que j'aie
être to be	sois soyons soyez	suis, es, est, sommes, êtes, sont	étais étant	serai serais	avoir été fus	que je sois
aller to go	va allons allez	vais, vas, va, allons, allez, vont	allais allant	irai irais	être allé(e) allai	que j'aille
apercevoir to notice	aperçois apercevons apercevez	aperçois, -ois, -oit, apercevons, -ez, aperçoivent	apercevais apercevant	apercevrai apercevrais	avoir aperçu aperçus	que j'aperçoive

Infinitive	Imperative	Present	Imperfect / Pres. participle	Future / Conditional	Past participle / Passé simple	Subjunctive
appeler to call	appelle appelons appelez	appelle, -es, -e, appelons, -ez, appellent	appelais appelant	appellerai appellerais	avoir appelé appelai	que j'appelle
s'asseoir to sit down	assieds-toi asseyons-nous asseyez-vous	assieds, -s, assied, asseyons, -ez, -ent	asseyais asseyant	assiérai assiérais	être assis(e) assis	que je m'asseye
battre to beat	bats battons battez	bats, -s, bat, battons, -ez, -ent	battais battant	battrai battrais	avoir battu battis	que je batte
boire to drink	bois buvons buvez	bois, -s, -t, buvons, -ez, boivent	buvais buvant	boirai boirais	avoir bu bus	que je boive
conduire to lead, drive	conduis conduisons conduisez	conduis, -s, it, conduisons, -ez, -ent	conduisais conduisant	conduirai conduirais	avoir conduit conduisis	que je conduise
connaître to know	connais connaissons connaissez	connais, -s, connaît, connaissons, -ez, -ent	connaissais connaissant	connaîtrai connaîtrais	avoir connu connus	que je connaisse
courir to run	cours courons courez	cours, -s, -t, courons, -ez, -ent	courais courant	courrai courrais	avoir couru courus	que je coure
craindre to fear	crains craignons craignez	crains, -s, -t, craignons, -ez, -ent	craignais craignant	craindrai craindrais	avoir craint craignis	que je craigne
croire to believe	crois croyons croyez	crois, -s, -t, croyons, -ez, croient	croyais croyant	croirai croirais	avoir cru crus	que je croie

Infinitive	Imperative	Present indicative	Imperfect / Pres. p.	Future / Conditional	Perfect / Past historic	Present subjunctive
cueillir to gather	cueille cueillons cueillez	cueille, -es, -e, cueillons, -ez, -ent	cueillais cueillant	cueillerai cueillerais	avoir cueilli cueillis	que je cueille
devoir to owe, have to	dois devons devez	dois, -s, -t, devons, -ez, doivent	devais devant	devrai devrais	avoir dû (f due) dus	que je doive
dire to say	dis disons dites	dis, -s, -t, disons, dites, disent	disais disant	dirai dirais	avoir dit dis	que je dise
dormir to sleep	dors dormons dormez	dors, -s, -t, dormons, -ez, -ent	dormait dormant	dormirai dormirais	avoir dormi dormis	que je dorme
écrire to write	écris écrivons écrivez	écris, -s, -t, écrivons, -ez, -ent	écrivais écrivant	écrirai écrirais	avoir écrit écrivis	que j'écrive
envoyer to send	envoie envoyons envoyez	envoie, -es, -e, envoyons, -ez, envoient	envoyais envoyant	enverrai enverrais	avoir envoyé envoyai	que j'envoie
espérer to hope	espère espérons espérez	espère, -es, -e, espérons, -ez, espèrent	espérais espérant	espérerai espérerais	avoir espéré espérai	que j'espère
faire to do, make	fais faisons faites	fais, -s, -t, faisons, faites, font	faisais faisant	ferai ferais	avoir fait fis	que je fasse

Infinitive		il faut	il fallait	il faudra / il faudrait	il a fallu / il fallut	qu'il faille
falloir to have to	—	—	—	il faudra il faudrait	il a fallu il fallut	—
fuir to flee	fuis fuyons fuyez	fuis, -s, -t, fuyons, -ez, fuient	fuyais fuyant	fuirai fuirais	avoir fui fuis	que je fuie
lire to read	lis lisons lisez	lis, -s, -t, lisons, -ez, -ent	lisais lisant	lirai lirais	avoir lu lus	que je lise
manger to eat	mange mangeons mangez	mange, -es, -e, mangeons, mangez, -ent	mangeais mangeant	mangerai mangerais	avoir mangé mangeai	que je mange
mettre to put	mets mettons mettez	mets, -s, met, mettons, -ez, -ent	mettais mettant	mettrai mettrais	avoir mis mis	que je mette
mourir to die	meurs mourons mourez	meurs, -s, -t, mourons, -ez, meurent	mourais mourant	mourrai mourrais	être mort(e) mourus	que je meure
naître to be born	nais naissons naissez	nais, -s, naît, naissons, -ez, -ent	naissais naissant	naîtrai naîtrais	être né(e) naquis	que je naisse
offrir to offer	offre offrons offrez	offre, -es, -e, offrons, -ez, -ent	offrais offrant	offrirai offrirais	avoir offert offris	que j'offre
ouvrir to open	ouvre ouvrons ouvrez	ouvre, -es, -e, ouvrons, -ez, -ent	ouvrais ouvrant	ouvrirai ouvrirais	avoir ouvert ouvris	que j'ouvre

Infinitive	Imperative	Present indicative	Imperfect Pres. p.	Future Conditional	Perfect Past historic	Present subjunctive
partir to leave	pars partons partez	pars, -s, -t, partons, -ez, -ent	partais partant	partirai partirais	être parti(e) partis	que je parte
plaire to please	plais plaisons plaisez	plais, -s, plaît, plaisons, -ez, -ent	plaisais plaisant	plairai plairais	avoir plu plus	que je plaise
pleuvoir to rain	—	il pleut	pleuvais pleuvant	il pleuvra il pleuvrait	il a plu il plut	qu'il pleuve
pouvoir to be able	—	peux (puis), -x, -t, pouvons, -ez, peuvent	pouvais pouvant	pourrai pourrais	avoir pu pus	que je puisse
prendre to take	prends prenons prenez	prends, -s, prend, prenons, -ez, prennent	prenais prenant	prendrai prendrais	avoir pris pris	que je prenne
recevoir to receive	reçois recevons recevez	reçois, -s, -t, recevons, -ez, reçoivent	recevais recevant	recevrai recevrais	avoir reçu reçus	que je reçoive
rire to laugh	ris rions riez	ris, -s, -t, rions, -ez, -ent	riais riant	rirai rirais	avoir ri ris	que je rie
rompre to break	romps rompons rompez	romps, -s, -t, rompons, -ez, -ent	rompais rompant	romprai romprais	avoir rompu rompis	que je rompe

savoir to know	sache sachons sachez	sais, -s, -t, savons, -ez, -ent	savais savant	saurai saurais	avoir su sus	que je sache
sentir to feel, smell	sens sentons sentez	sens, -s, -t, sentons, -ez, -ent	sentais sentant	sentirai sentirais	avoir senti sentis	que je sente
sortir to go out	sors sortons sortez	sors, -s, -t, sortons, -ez, -ent	sortais sortant	sortirai sortirais	être sorti(e) sortis	que je sorte
suivre to follow	suis suivons suivez	suis, -s, -t, suivons, -ez, -ent	suivais suivant	suivrai suivrais	avoir suivi suivis	que je suive
se taire to be silent	tais-toi taisons-nous taisez-vous	tais, -s, -t, taisons, -ez, -ent	taisais taisant	tairai tairais	être tu(e) tus	que je taise
tenir to hold	tiens tenons tenez	tiens, -s, -t, tenons, -ez, tiennent	tenais tenant	tiendrai tiendrais	avoir tenu tins	que je tienne
valoir to be worth	vaux valons valez	vaux, -x, vaut, valons, -ez, -ent	valais valant	vaudrai vaudrais	avoir valu valus	que je vaille
venir to come	viens venons venez	viens, -s, -t, venons, -ez, viennent	venais venant	viendrai viendrais	être venu(e) vins	que je vienne
vivre to live	vis vivons vivez	vis, -s, -t, vivons, -ez, -ent	vivais vivant	vivrai vivrais	avoir vécu vécus	que je vive

Infinitive	Imperative	Present indicative	Imperfect Pres. p.	Future Conditional	Perfect Past historic	Present subjunctive
voir to see	vois voyons voyez	vois, -s, -t, voyons, -ez, voient	voyais voyant	verrai verrais	avoir vu vis	que je voie
vouloir to wish, want	veuille veuillons veuillez	veux, -x, -t, voulons, -ez, veulent	voulais voulant	voudrai voudrais	avoir voulu voulus	que je veuille

PART TWO

READING PASSAGES AND VOCABULARY

■ READING PASSAGES AND TRANSLATIONS

1

Cet après-midi, à l'école, on n'a pas rigolé, parce que le directeur est venu en classe nous distribuer les carnets. Il n'avait pas l'air content le directeur quand il est entré avec nos carnets sous le bras. 'Je suis dans l'enseignement depuis des années, il a dit le directeur, et je n'ai jamais vu une classe aussi dissipée. Les observations portées sur vos carnets par votre maîtresse en font foi. Je vais commencer à distribuer les carnets.'

Et Clotaire s'est mis à pleurer. Clotaire c'est le dernier de la classe et tous les mois, dans son carnet, la maîtresse écrit des tas de choses et le papa et la maman ne sont pas contents et le privent de dessert et de télévision. Ils sont tellement habitués, m'a raconté Clotaire, qu'une fois par mois, sa maman ne fait pas de dessert et son papa va voir la télévision chez des voisins.

Sur mon carnet à moi il y avait: 'Élève turbulent, souvent distrait. Pourrait faire mieux.' Eudes avait: 'Élève dissipé. Se bat avec ses camarades. Pourrait faire mieux.' Pour Rufus, c'était: 'Persiste à jouer en classe avec un sifflet à roulette, maintes fois confisqué. Pourrait faire mieux.' Le seul qui ne pouvait faire mieux c'était Agnan. Agnan c'est le premier de la classe et le chouchou de la maîtresse. Le directeur nous a lu le carnet d'Agnan: 'Élève appliqué, intelligent. Arrivera.' Le directeur nous a dit qu'on devait suivre l'exemple d'Agnan, que nous étions des petits vauriens, que nous finirons au bagne et que ça ferait sûrement beaucoup de peine à nos papas et à nos mamans qui devaient avoir d'autres projets pour nous. Et puis il est parti.

(Sempé-Goscinny)

This afternoon, at school, it was no joke because the headmaster came into class to give us our reports. He didn't look happy, the headmaster, when he came in with our reports under his arm. 'I have been in teaching for years,' the headmaster said, 'and I have never seen such an inattentive class. The remarks made on your reports by your teacher bear witness to this. I am going to start giving out the reports.'

And Clotaire began to cry. Clotaire is bottom of the class and every month, on his report, teacher writes a load of things and his mum and dad are not pleased and they don't let him have any pudding or television. They're so used to it, Clotaire told me, that once a month his mum doesn't make any pudding and his dad goes next door to watch television.

On my report there was: 'Disruptive pupil, often inattentive. Could do better.' Eudes had: 'Inattentive pupil. Fights with his classmates. Could do better.' For Rufus there was: 'Persistently plays in class with a whistle, often confiscated. Could do better.' The only one who couldn't do better was Agnan. Agnan is top of the class and teacher's pet. The headmaster read us Agnan's report: 'Hardworking pupil, intelligent. Will go far.' The head-master told us that we should follow Agnan's example, that we were little good-for-nothings, that we would end up in prison and that this would certainly distress our mums and dads who must have other plans for us. And then he left.

2

– Entrez donc! dit M. Thuillier.

– Je ne voudrais pas vous déranger . . .

– Quelle idée! J'avais fini de travailler! J'habite seul! Et je n'attends personne! Autant dire que vous tombez bien . . .

Étienne pénétra dans une petite pièce basse et sale, qui lui parut taillée dans du mauvais carton. Une lampe de bureau, coiffée d'un abat-jour vert absinthe, versait une lueur sous-marine sur des récifs de livres à demi éboulés et des dalles de papier blanc. L'air était saturé d'une odeur épaisse de tabac. Une large planche, placée sur des tréteaux, servait de table.

– Asseyez-vous dit M. Thuillier en désignant un fauteuil en rotin.

Lui-même restait debout, les mains dans les poches, le bedon en avant. Il était en manches de chemise, la cravate nouée bas. Deux cellules d'or marquaient les verres bombés de ses lunettes. Un mégot éteint pendait à sa lèvre. Étienne respirait avec difficulté. Tout au fond de lui, sous de lourdes couches de chair inerte, il sentait battre son cœur. Un vertige se leva du parquet nu et souillé de cendres. 'Je vais vomir,' pensa Étienne.

– Quoi de neuf? demanda M. Thuillier.

Étienne se pencha un peu. Le fauteuil grinça.

– J'ai besoin de vous, monsieur, dit Etienne d'une voix contenue.

M. Thuillier ne le quittait pas du regard:

– Ah! Oui?

– Oui . . . Il faut que je vous dise . . . c'est . . . très grave.

Il se tut. Les mots se bloquaient dans sa gorge. Une chaleur de honte courait sur sa peau. M. Thuillier inclina la tête et tenta de rallumer son mégot à la flamme d'un briquet rond et plat:

– Vous avez des ennuis?

– Oui, dit Étienne.

– Quels ennuis?

Étienne hésita quelques secondes, ferma à demi les paupières et répondit dans un souffle:

– Tout à l'heure, j'ai voulu me suicider.

– Mes compliments, dit M. Thuillier.

(Troyat)

'Come in,' said Mr Thuillier.

'I wouldn't want to disturb you . . .'

'What an idea! I'd finished working. I live alone! And I'm not expecting anyone! In other words, you come at a good time . . .'

Stephen went into a low, dirty little room which seemed to him to be fashioned out of poor quality cardboard. A desk lamp covered by an absinthe-green shade shed a submarine light over half-caved-in reefs of books and flagstones of white paper. The air was impregnated with a thick smell of tobacco. A broad plank placed on trestles served as a table.

'Sit down', said Mr Thuillier, motioning towards a cane chair.

He himself remained standing with his hands in his pockets and his stomach sticking out. He was in shirtsleeves with his tie loosely knotted. Two golden circles outlined the bulging lenses of his spectacles. A dog-end hung from his lip. Stephen was having difficulty breathing. Deep inside him, under heavy layers of inert flesh, he could feel his heart beating. Dizziness rose up from the bare ash-soiled floor. 'I'm going to be sick,' Stephen thought.

'What's new?' asked Mr Thuillier.

'Stephen leaned forward slightly. The chair creaked.

'I need you, sir', Stephen said in a constrained voice.

Mr Thuillier did not take his eyes off him:

'Oh yes?'

'Yes . . . I have to tell you . . . it's . . . very serious.'

He was silent. The words stuck in his throat. A flush of shame spread over his skin. Mr Thuillier bent forward and tried to re-kindle his dog-end in the flame of a round, flat cigarette lighter.

'Do you have problems?'

'Yes,' said Stephen.

'What problems?'

Stephen hesitated a few moments, half-closed his eyelids and replied in one breath, 'Just now, I wanted to kill myself.'

'Congratulations,' said Mr Thuillier.

3

Les faibles touches de l'aube détachèrent les branches pendantes, les feuillages noirs. Ce n'était pas une route, tout au plus un chemin de forêt. On avait dû s'arrêter dans les derniers arbres, et sur la droite déjà des enclos de cultures beiges et rayeés trahissaient l'approche de l'homme. On passait juste entre les haies avec les camions. L'énorme chenille morcelée, immobile, gelait de fatigue dans cette première clarté. Des officiers se frappaient les bras, battant le sol de la semelle, remontaient la colonne, plus par énervement que parce qu'ils avaient un devoir à remplir. Au passage, des visages sortaient des voitures. Tout cela était gris, couleur d'insomnie, interrogateur. Les dragons entassés sous les bâches parlaient entre eux à voix basse, et le métal commençait à luire, les armes, les gamelles. Qu'est-ce qu'on attendait? Sait-on jamais? On suit la voiture qui est devant, voilà tout. Ces déplacements de nuit, c'est tuant, surtout à cause de la lenteur. Ne descendez pas, nom de Dieu! Les véhicules à ce niveau-ci étaient flanqués de motocyclistes, de side-cars. Une infiltration de roues et de bonhommes. Un aspirant dormait dans son side; les trous de nez au ciel, la gueule ouverte, et pâle comme l'heure. Les autres sur leurs selles, le fusil à l'épaule, tombaient de sommeil. Plusieurs avaient piqué leur somme assis, le corps cassé. D'autres, profitant de la halte, la roue calée, s'étaient couchés sur leur engin comme dans un berceau, la nuque sur leur selle, les pieds au guidon. Des hommes jeunes, le casque à ce point vissé sur la tête qu'ils ne pouvaient plus dormir sans lui. Des hommes de cuir et de métal, où l'on s'étonnait à l'aurore de voir que la barbe avait poussé.

(Aragon)

The faint hints of dawn picked out the hanging branches, the black foliage. It wasn't a road; at best a forest track. They had had to stop among the last trees and already, on the right, plots of fawn, furrowed land betrayed humanity's approach. The trucks just managed to get through between the hedges. The enormous caterpillar, disjointed and motionless, lay exhausted and freezing in that early light. Officers, stamping on the ground, beating their arms, went back up the column more from apprehension than because they had a duty to carry out. As they went past, faces poked out of the vehicles. It was all grey; a sleepless questioning colour. The dragoons, huddled together under the tarpaulins, muttered among themselves in undertones, and the metal of the weapons, of the mess-tins, began to glint. What were they waiting for? You're never told. All you do is follow the truck in front. These night manoeuvres are killing, mainly because they drag on. For Christ's sake don't get out! The vehicles at this point were flanked by motorbikes and sidecars. A tangle of blokes and wheels. A cadet was asleep in his side-car; nostrils in the air; gob open, pale as the early light. The others on their saddles, rifles slung, were dead tired. Several of them had grabbed a nap sitting down, bodies slumped. Others, taking advantage of the stop, their wheels wedged, were lying on their machines, the backs of their necks on the saddles, their feet on the handlebars, as if they were in cradles.

Young men, their helmets so firmly screwed on to their heads that they couldn't sleep without them any more; men of leather and metal on whom, as dawn broke, you were surprised to see that stubble had grown.

■ OTHER PASSAGES FOR READING

MAXIMES

31 Si nous n'avions pas de défauts, nous ne prendrions pas tant de plaisir à en remarquer dans les autres.

56 Pour s'établir dans le monde, on fait tout ce que l'on peut pour y paraître établi.

84 Il est plus honteux de se défier de ses amis que d'en être trompé.

89 Tout le monde se plaint de sa mémoire, et personne ne se plaint de son jugement.

93 Les vieillards aiment à donner de bons préceptes pour se consoler de n'être plus en état de donner de mauvais exemples.

94 Les défauts de l'esprit augmentent en vieillissant, comme ceux du visage.

138 On aime mieux dire du mal de soi-même que de n'en point parler.

168 L'espérance, toute trompeuse qu'elle est, sert au moins à nous mener à la fin de la vie par un chemin agréable.

347 Nous ne trouvons guère de gens de bon sens que ceux qui sont de notre avis.

372 La plupart des jeunes gens croient être naturels lorsqu'ils ne sont que mal polis et grossiers.

431 Rien n'empêche tant d'être naturel que l'envie de le paraître.

461 La vieillesse est un tyran qui défend sur peine de la vie tous les plaisirs de la jeunesse.

110 On ne donne rien si libéralement que ses conseils.

(La Rochefoucauld)

La Musique

La musique souvent me prend comme une mer!
   Vers ma pâle étoile,
Sous un plafond de brume ou dans un vaste éther
   Je mets à la voile;

La poitrine en avant et les poumons gonflés
   Comme de la toile,
J'escalade le dos des flots amoncelés
   Que la nuit me voile;

Je sens vibrer en moi toutes les passions
   D'un vaisseau qui souffre;
Le bon vent, la tempête et ses convulsions

   Sur l'immense gouffre
Me bercent. – D'autres fois, calme plat, grand miroir
   De mon désespoir!

               (Baudelaire)

'Il pleut doucement sur la ville'—Arthur Rimbaud

Il pleure dans mon cœur
Comme il pleut sur la ville;
Quelle est cette langueur
Qui pénètre mon cœur?

O bruit doux de la pluie
Par terre et sur les toits!
Pour un cœur qui s'ennuie
O le chant de la pluie!

Il pleure sans raison
Dans ce cœur qui s'écœure.
Quoi! nulle trahison?
Ce deuil est sans raison.

C'est bien la pire peine
De ne savoir pourquoi

Sans amour et sans haine
Mon cœur a tant de peine!
                    (Verlaine)

Le Pont Mirabeau

Sous le pont Mirabeau coule la Seine
        Et nos amours
    Faut-il qu'il m'en souvienne
La joie venait toujours après la peine

        Vienne la nuit sonne l'heure
        Les jours s'en vont je demeure

Les mains dans les mains restons face à face
        Tandis que sous
    Le pont de nos bras passe
Des éternels regards l'onde si lasse

        Vienne la nuit sonne l'heure
        Les jours s'en vont je demeure

L'amour s'en va comme cette eau courante
        L'amour s'en va
    Comme la vie est lente
Et comme l'espérance est violente

        Vienne la nuit sonne l'heure
        Les jours s'en vont je demeure

Passe les jours et passent les semaines
        Ni temps passé
    Ni les amours reviennent
Sous le pont Mirabeau coule la Seine

        Vienne la nuit sonne l'heure
        Les jours s'en vont je demeure
                            (Apollinaire)

VOCABULARY

The following is merely a guide to some French equivalents of common English words. It is not a complete answer to problems of translation and must be used in conjunction with a careful study of the previous chapters.

to abandon: abandonner
to be able (to): pouvoir
about (=approx.): environ; à
    peu près
    (=around): autour de
    (=concerning): à propos
    de
to be about to: être sur le
  point de
above: au-dessus de
abroad: à l'étranger
absolute (-ly): absolu
  (absolument)
accent: l'accent (m)
accident: l'accident (m)
according to: selon
account: le compte
across: à travers
actually: vraiment;
  effectivement
to add: ajouter
address: l'adresse (f)
to admire: admirer
to advise: conseiller
to be afraid (of): avoir peur
  (de)
Africa: l'Afrique (f)
after: après; au bout de
afternoon: l'après-midi (m)
again: de nouveau
once again: encore une fois

against: contre
age: l'âge (m)
to age: vieillir
(a month) ago: il y a (un mois)
air: l'air (m)
airport: l'aéroport (m)
all: tout, toute, tous, toutes
not at all: pas du tout
to allow: permettre
almost: presque
alone: seul
along: le long de
Alps: les Alpes (f)
already: déjà
also: aussi
although: bien que, quoique
  (+ subj.)
always: toujours
American: américain
among: parmi
angry: fâché; en colère
to get angry: se fâcher
in any case: en tout cas
anywhere: ne . . . nulle part
appetite: l'appétit (m)
animal: l'animal (m); la bête
answer: la réponse
to answer: répondre
apart from: à part
to apologise: s'excuser
to appear: paraître

appointment: le rendez-vous
to approach: s'approcher (de)
to argue: discuter
arm: le bras
armchair: le fauteuil
around: autour de
to arrange: arranger
arrival: l'arrivée (f)
to arrive: arriver
as (though): comme (si)
as much as: autant que
as soon as: dès que; aussitôt que
to ask: demander
to ask a question: poser une question
to be asleep: dormir
to fall asleep: s'endormir
to astonish: étonner
astonished: étonné
at once: tout de suite
attempt: la tentative
to attend: assister (à)
attention: l'attention (f)
aunt: la tante
Austria: l'Autriche (f)
autumn: l'automne (m)
to avoid (doing something): éviter (de faire quelque chose)
to await: attendre
(100km) away: à (cent k)
to go away: s'en aller
awful: affreux

back: le dos
back (a car): faire reculer
bad (-ly): mauvais (mal)
bag: le sac

baker: le boulanger
bank (=money): la banque (=river): la rive
bar: le bar
bare: nu
basket: la corbeille
to bathe: se baigner
bathroom: la salle de bains
beach: la plage
to beat: battre
beautiful: beau (belle)
because: parce que
because of: à cause de
to become: devenir
bed: le lit
bedroom: la chambre
beef: le boeuf
before (time): avant de (place): devant
the day before: la veille
to begin: commencer; se mettre à
beginning: le commencement; le début
to behave: se comporter
behind: derrière
to believe: croire
to belong (to): appartenir (à)
below: au-dessous de
belt: la ceinture
beside: à côté de
better (adj.): meilleur (adv.): mieux
between: entre
beyond: au delà de
bicycle: la bicyclette; le vélo
big: grand; gros (-se)
bill (in café, shop, etc.): le compte; l'addition (f)

bird: l'oiseau (m)
bit (of): le morceau; un bout de; un peu de
black: noir
blanket: la couverture
blue: bleu (-e)
boat: le bateau
body: le corps
bone: l'os (m)
book: le livre
to book (seat, etc.): retenir
to bore (be bored): ennuyer; (s'ennuyer)
to be born: naître
to borrow (from): emprunter (à)
boss: le patron
both: tous (toutes) les deux
bottle: la bouteille
at the bottom (of): au fond (de)
boy: le garçon
box: la boîte
to brake: freiner
brave: courageux (-se)
bread: le pain
to break: casser; briser; rompre
breakfast: le petit déjeuner
to breathe: respirer
bridge: le pont
briefcase: la serviette
to bring (things or people): apporter; amener
to bring back (things or people): rapporter; ramener
to bring (carry) down: descendre
British: britannique

broad: large
brother: le frère
brown: brun
to build: bâtir; construire
building: le batîment; un immeuble
bus: un autobus
business: les affaires (f)
busy: occupé
but: mais
butcher: le boucher
butter: le beurre
to buy: acheter
by: par
    (=near): près de

cake: le gâteau (-x)
to call: appeler
to be called: s'appeler
calm: calme; tranquille
camera: l'appareil (m) photo
can (to be able to): pouvoir
    (to know how to): savoir
Canada: le Canada
car: la voiture; la bagnole
to be careful: faire attention à
caretaker: le (la) concierge·
carpet: le tapis
to carry: porter
to carry away: emporter
case (suitcase): la valise
cat: le chat
to catch: attraper
to cease (doing): cesser (de faire)
centimetre: le centimètre
centre: le centre
century: le siècle
certain (-ly): certain (-ement)

chair: la chaise; le fauteuil
change (money): la monnaie
to change: changer
charming: charmant
to chat: causer; bavarder
cheap: peu cher; bon marché
to cheat: tricher
cheek: la joue
cheese: le fromage
chemist's shop: la pharmacie
chest: la poitrine
chicken: le poulet
chief (adj.): principal
child: un(e) enfant; le (la) gosse
chips (potato): les frites (f)
to choose: choisir
Christmas: le Noël
church: une église
cigar: le cigare
cigarette: la cigarette
cinema: le cinéma
city: la ville; la grande ville; la
   cité
class: la classe
clean: propre
to clean: nettoyer
clear: clair
clever: intelligent
client: le client
to climb: grimper
clock (small): la pendule
   (outdoor): l'horloge (f)
to close: fermer
close to: près de
clothes: les vêtements (m)
cloud: le nuage
coast: la côte
coat (man): le pardessus
   (woman): le manteau

coffee: le café
cold: froid
colour: la couleur
to come: venir
to come back: revenir
to come down: descendre
to come home: rentrer
to come in: entrer
to come out: sortir
to come up: monter
comfortable: confortable;
   être à l'aise
compartment: le compartiment
to complain (about): se
   plaindre (de)
completely: complètement;
   tout à fait
to consider: considérer
to contain: contenir
to continue (to): continuer (à)
corner: le coin
corridor: le couloir
cost: le prix
to count: compter
counter: le comptoir
country: le pays
the country: la campagne
countryside: le paysage
of course: bien entendu;
   évidemment; naturellement
cousin: le (la) cousin(e)
to cover: couvrir
cow: la vache
crazy: fou (folle)
crisps: les chips (m)
to cross: traverser
crossroads: le croisement; le
   carrefour
crowd: la foule

cruel: cruel (-lle)
to cry: pleurer
to cry out: s'écrier
cup: la tasse
cupboard: le placard
curtain: le rideau
customer: le client
customs: la douane
customs official: le douanier
to cut: couper
cyclist: le cycliste

dance: le bal
to dance: danser
dangerous: dangereux (-se)
dark: sombre; noir
daughter: la fille
day: le jour; la journée
day after: le lendemain
day before: la veille
dead: mort (e)
dear: cher (-ère)
to decide (to): décider (de)
deck: le pont
declare: déclarer
deep: profond
deliberately: exprès
dentist: le dentiste
departure: le départ
describe: décrire
deserted: désert
desk: le bureau
destination: la destination
to destroy: détruire
to dial (telephone): composer
to die: mourir
diesel: le gas-oil
different: différent
difficult: difficile

difficulty: la difficulté
to dine: dîner
dining-room: la salle à manger
dinner: le dîner
direction: la direction; (traffic)
   le sens
dirty: sale
to disappear: disparaître
to discover: découvrir
to discuss: discuter
distance: la distance
in the distance: au loin
district: le quartier
to disturb: déranger
to do: faire
doctor: le médecin
dog: le chien
door: la porte
doubt: le doute
doubtless: sans doute
down (=below): en bas
dozen: la douzaine
drawer: le tiroir
dreadful: affreux
dream: le rêve
to dream: rêver
dress: la robe
to dress: s'habiller
dressing-gown: la robe de
   chambre
drink: le boisson
to drink: boire
to drive (car): conduire
driver: le conducteur; le
   chauffeur
to drop: laisser tomber
dry: sec (-èche)
to dry: sécher
duck: le canard

during: pendant

each (adj.): chaque
   (pron.): chacun
early: de bonne heure; tôt
to earn: gagner
earth: la terre
east: l'est (m)
easy (-ily): facile (-ment)
to eat: manger
edge: le bord
egg: un oeuf
electric: éléctrique
elsewhere: ailleurs
empty: vide
end: la fin; le bout
to end: finir; terminer
engaged (e.g. toilets): occupé
engine (car): le moteur
England: l'Angleterre (f)
English: anglais
to enjoy oneself: s'amuser
enough: assez
to enter: entrer (dans)
entirely: tout à fait
entrance: l'entrée (f)
envelope: une enveloppe
equal (-ly): égal (-ement)
to escape: échapper
especially: surtout
Europe: l'Europe (f)
even: même
evening: le soir; la soirée
event: un événement
eventually: enfin
ever: jamais
every: chaque; tout
everybody: tout le monde
   (+ sing. verb)

every day: tous les jours
everywhere: partout
to examine: examiner
except: sauf
to excuse oneself: s'excuser
exit: la sortie
to expect: attendre
expensive: cher (-ère)
to explain: expliquer
explanation: une explication
extraordinary: extraordinaire
eye: un oeil (les yeux)

face: le visage; la figure
facing: en face de
factory: une usine
fairly: assez
to fall: tomber
to fall asleep: s'endormir
false: faux (-sse)
family: la famille
famous: célèbre
far (from): loin (de)
farm: la ferme
farmer: le fermier
fast: rapide; vite
to fasten: attacher
fat: gros; gras
father: le père
fault: la faute
fear: la peur
to fear: avoir peur (de)
to feel: sentir; ressentir
feeling: le sentiment
to fetch: aller chercher
few; a few: peu (de); quelques
field: le champ
to fight: se battre
to fill: remplir

finally: enfin
to find: trouver
to find out: découvrir
fine: beau (bel) (belle)
finger: le doigt
to finish: finir; terminer
fire: le feu
first: premier (-ière)
at first: d'abord
fish: le poisson
to fish: pêcher
fishing: la pêche
flat: un appartement
flat: plat
floor: le plancher; le parquet
    (storey of building): un
        étage
ground floor: le rez-de-chaussée
flower: la fleur
fluent (-ly): courant
   (couramment)
to fly: voler
fog: le brouillard
to follow: suivre
foot: le pied
football: le foot(bal)
for: pour
    (time): pendant; depuis
forehead: le front
foreigner: un(e) étranger (-ère)
forest: la forêt
to forget: oublier
to forgive (someone):
   pardonner (à quelqu'un)
fortnight: la quinzaine
fortunately: heureusement
France: la France
free: libre
to freeze: geler

French: français
fresh: frais (fraîche)
friend: un(e) ami(e); le copain
   (la copine)
to frighten: effrayer
from: de
in front of: devant
frontier: la frontière
fruit: le fruit
full: plein
to make fun (of): se moquer
   (de)
furniture: les meubles
further: plus loin

garage: le garage
garden: le jardin
gate: la porte; la barrière
to gather: cueillir
generous: généreux(-se)
gentleman: le monsieur
gently: doucement
German: allemand
Germany: l'Allemagne (f)
to get into: monter dans
to get out: sortir; descendre
to get up: se lever
gift: le cadeau
girl: la fille
to give: donner
to give back: rendre
glad: content: heureux(-se)
glass: le verre
glasses: les lunettes (f)
glove: le gant
to go: aller; (of machines)
   marcher
to go across: traverser
to go away: s'en aller

to go down: descendre
to go in: entrer (dans)
to go to bed: se coucher
to go out: sortir; (e.g. lights) s'éteindre
good: bon(-nne)
good-bye: au revoir; adieu
goods: la marchandise
gradually: peu à peu
grandfather: le grand-père
grandmother: la grand'mère
grass: l'herbe (f)
great: grand
green: vert
grey: gris
guest: un(e) invité(e)

hairdresser: le coiffeur
half: la moitié
hall: le vestibule
hand: la main
handbag: le sac à main
handkerchief: le mouchoir
to happen: arriver; se passer
happy: heureux (-se)
harbour: le port
hard: dur; difficile
hardly: à peine; ne . . . guère
to harm: faire du mal à
hat: le chapeau
to have: avoir
to have just: venir de
to have to: devoir; il faut
head: la tête
headlight: la phare
to hear: entendre
heart: le cœur
heavy: lourd
hedge: la haie

to help: aider; donner un coup de main (à)
here: ici
here is (are): voici
to hesitate: hésiter
to hide: se cacher
high: haut
hill: la colline
to hire: louer
to hit: frapper
to hold: tenir
hole: le trou
holiday: les vacances (f)
at home: chez (moi, etc.)
to hope: espérer
horse: le cheval (-aux)
hot: chaud
hotel: l'hôtel (m)
hour: l'heure (f)
house: la maison
how: comment
however: cependant
how much: combien (de)
hunger: la faim
to be hungry: avoir faim
to hurry: se dépêcher
to be in a hurry: être pressé
husband: le mari

idea: l'idée (f)
if: si
ill: malade
immediately: immédiatement; tout de suite
industrial: industriel (-lle)
information: les renseignements (m)
inhabitant: l'habitant (m)
inside: l'intérieur (m)

to insist: insister
inspector (tickets): le contrôleur
instead (of): au lieu (de) (+ inf.)
to insure: assurer
intelligent: intelligent
to intend (to): avoir l'intention (de)
to be interested (in): s'intéresser (à)
to interrupt: interrompre
to invite: inviter
Ireland: l'Irelande (f)
Italy: l'Italie (f)

jacket: le veston
jewel: le bijou
job: le métier; un emploi; un job
to joke: plaisanter; rigoler
journey: le voyage
to jump: sauter
to have just (done): venir de (faire)
just now: tout à l'heure

to keep: garder
kerb: le bord du trottoir
key: la clef
to kick: donner un coup de pied (à)
to kill: tuer
kilometre: le kilomètre
kind: la sorte
    (adj.): gentil (-lle); aimable
king: le roi
kitchen: la cuisine

knee: le genou (-x)
knife: le couteau
to knock over: renverser
to know: savoir; connaître

lack: le (un) manque (de)
lads: les gars
lady: la dame
lake: le lac
lamb: l'agneau (m)
land: la terre
to land: atterrir
language: la langue
large: grand
last: dernier (-ère)
last night: hier soir
at last: enfin
late: tard; en retard
to laugh: rire
lavatory: les cabinets (m); les toilettes (f)
lazy: paresseux (-se)
to lead: mener; conduire
leader: le chef
leaf: la feuille
to leap: sauter
to learn (to): apprendre (à)
least (adj.): le (la) moindre
    (adv.): le moins
at least: au moins
to leave: quitter; partir; laisser
left: (la) gauche
to have left: il (me, etc.) reste
leg: la jambe
lemonade: la limonade
to lend: prêter
less: moins
to let: laisser; (e.g. rooms) louer

to let go: lâcher
letter: la lettre
library: la bibliothèque
to lie down: se coucher;
  s'étendre
life: la vie
lift: un ascenseur
to lift: lever
light: la lumière
    (adj.): léger (-ère)
to light: allumer
lightning: l'éclair (m)
like: comme
to like: aimer
to be like: ressembler (à)
line: la ligne
lip: la lèvre
list: la liste
to listen to: écouter
litre: le litre
little; a little: petit; un peu
to live: vivre
to live in: habiter
lively: vif (-ve)
to load: charger
lock: la serrure
London: Londres
long (adj.): long (-ue)
    (adv.): longtemps
how long: combien de temps
no longer: ne . . . plus
to look (=appear): paraître;
  avoir l'air
to look at: regarder
to look for: chercher
to look up: lever les yeux
lorry: le camion
to lose: perdre
a lot (of): beaucoup (de)

loud(ly): fort; à haute voix
love: l'amour (m)
to love: aimer
low: bas (-sse)
to lower: baisser
to be lucky: avoir de la chance
luggage: les bagages (f)
a lump (of): un morceau (de)
lunch: le déjeuner
to have lunch: déjeuner

mad: fou (-lle)
magnificent: magnifique
mail (post): le courrier
to make: faire
man: un homme
manager: le directeur
mantelpiece: la cheminée
many: beaucoup (de)
how many (much): combien
  (de)
too many (much): trop (de)
so many (much): tant (de)
as many (much) . . . as: autant
  . . . que
map: la carte
mark (stain): la tache
market: le marché
marvellous: merveilleux (-se)
master: le maître
(school)master: le prof(esseur)
match: le match; l'allumette (f)
what's the matter?: qu'est-ce
  qu'il y a?
maybe: peut-être
may I (do)?: puis-je (faire)?
mayor: le maire
meal: le repas
to mean: vouloir dire

means: le moyen
meanwhile: pendant ce temps
meat: la viande
Mediterranean: la Méditerranée
to meet: rencontrer
menu: la carte
middle: le milieu
milk: le lait
mind out!: attention!
mine: le mien
minute: la minute
miserable: malheureux (-se)
to miss: manquer
mist: le brouillard; la brume
mistake: la faute; une erreur
to make a mistake (about): se tromper (de)
moment: le moment; un instant
money: l'argent (m)
moon: la lune
more: plus (de); davantage
no more: ne . . . plus
more and more: de plus en plus
more or less: plus ou moins
morning: le matin; la matinée
most (of): la plupart (de)
mother: la mère
motionless: immobile
motor: le moteur
motor car: la voiture; l'auto
mountain: la montagne
mouth: la bouche
to move: bouger
to move away: s'éloigner
movement: le mouvement
much: beaucoup (de)
mud: la boue

music: la musique
musician: le musicien
must (do): devoir (faire)

naked: nu
name: le nom
my name is . . . : je m'appelle . . .
narrow: étroit
nature: la nature
near: près de
nearly: presque
necessary: nécessaire
necklace: le collier
to need: avoir besoin (de)
neighbour: le voisin
neighbourhood: le quartier
neither . . . nor: ni . . . ni . . . ne
nephew: le neveu
nest: le nid
never: ne . . . jamais
new: nouveau
brand new: neuf (-ve)
New Year: le Nouvel An
news: les nouvelles (f)
the news: les informations (f)
newspaper: le journal
next: prochain
next (=then): puis; ensuite
next day: le lendemain
next to: à côté de
nice: aimable; gentil (-lle); joli
niece: la nièce
night: la nuit
last night: hier soir
no: non
nobody: ne . . . personne
nobody else: personne d'autre

noise: le bruit
noisy: bruyant
noon: midi (m)
north: le nord
northern: de nord
nothing: ne . . . rien
notice: un avis
to notice: remarquer
novel: le roman
now: maintenant
nowhere: ne . . . nulle part
number: le nombre; le numéro
numerous: nombreux(-se)
nurse: l'infirmière (f)

to obey: obéir
object: un objet
to be obliged to (do): être
    obligé de (faire)
to observe: observer;
    remarquer
obvious (-ly): évident
    (évidemment)
occasionally: de temps en
    temps
odd: étrange; bizarre
to offer: offrir
office: le bureau
    (=position): fonction (f)
often: souvent
old (=elderly): vieux; âgé
    (=former): ancien (-ne)
on (upon): sur
once: une fois
once more: encore une fois
at once: tout de suite
one: un(e)
the one who: celui (celle) qui
one (pron.): on

only (adj.): seul
    (adv.): seulement; ne
    . . . que
to open: ouvrir
opinion: un avis
in my opinion: à mon avis
opportunity: l'occasion (f)
opposite: en face de
or: ou
to order (goods): commander
other: autre
(e.g. I) ought to: devoir
ours: le nôtre
outside: dehors; à l'extérieur
    (m)
outskirts: les faubourgs (m)
over: fini; terminé
    (=above): au-dessus de
over there (here): là-bas (par
    ici)
overcoat: le pardessus
to overtake: doubler
to owe: devoir
own: propre
owner: le (la) propriétaire; le
    patron (la patronne)

packet: le paquet
page: la page
pain: la douleur
pale: pâle
palm-tree: le palmier
parcel: le paquet
parents: les parents (m)
park: le parc
to park: stationner
part: la partie
to pass: passer; (overtake)
    doubler

passenger: la passager; le voyageur

passer-by: le (la) passant(-e)

passport: le passeport

past: le passé

path: le sentier; l'allée (f)

pavement: le trottoir

to pay: payer

to pay attention: faire attention

peace: la paix

peasant: le paysan(-nne)

pen: le stylo

pencil: le crayon

people: les gens (m)

pepper: le poivre

perfect: parfait

perhaps: peut-être

perm: une permanente

to permit: permettre

person: la personne

petrol: l'essence (f)

to phone: téléphoner

photograph: la photo(graphie)

to pick: cueillir

to pick up: ramasser

picture: le tableau

piece: le morceau

pile: le tas

pink: rose

pipe (smoker's): la pipe

what a pity!: quel dommage!

place: l'endroit (m); le lieu

to take place: avoir lieu

plate: l'assiette (f)

platform: le quai

to play (football): jouer (au foot)
(the violin): jouer (du violon)

pleasant: agréable

to please (someone): plaire (à qu'un)

Please: S'il vous plaît; prière de

pleasure: le plaisir

plenty: beaucoup de

plus: en plus

pocket: la poche

to be on the point of: être sur le point de

policeman: un agent; le policier; le gendarme

polite: poli

poor: pauvre

porter: le porteur

possible: possible

post (=mail): le courrier

to post: mettre une lettre à la poste

post office: la Poste

postcard: une carte postale

postman: le facteur

potato: la pomme de terre

pound (weight): la livre

to pour: verser

powerful: puissant

to prefer: préférer; aimer mieux

to prepare: présenter

present: le cadeau

at present: actuellement

to present: présenter

pretty: joli

to prevent: empêcher

price: le prix

prison: le prison

probable (-ly): probable (-ment)

problem: le problème

product: le produit
to promise: promettre
provided that: pourvu que
public: public (-que)
punch: le coup de poing
to punish: punir
to pursue: poursuivre
to push: pousser
to put: mettre
to put out (e.g. lights):
  éteindre

quality: la qualité
quarter: le quart
a quarter of an hour: un quart
  d'heure
question: la question
it's a question of . . .: il s'agit
  de . . .
quick: vite
quickly: vite; rapidement
quiet: tranquille; calme;
  silencieux(-se)
to be quiet (silent): se taire
quietly: doucement
speak quietly: parler à voix
  basse
quite: tout à fait

rabbit: le lapin
radio: la radio
railway: le chemin de fer; la
  SNCF
railway line: la voie ferrée
to rain: pleuvoir
raincoat: l'imperméable (m)
to raise: lever
rapid: rapide
rarely: rarement

rather: assez
to reach: arriver à; atteindre
to read: lire
real: réel (-lle)
to realise: se rendre compte
really: vraiment
to receive: recevoir
recent: récent
reception (desk): la réception
to recognise: reconnaître
red: rouge
to refuse (to): refuser (de)
to regret: regretter
relatives: les parents (m)
to release: lâcher
to remain: rester
to remark: remarquer
to remember: se souvenir de
to remove: enlever
to repair: réparer
to repeat: répéter
to reply: répondre
to respond: répondre
responsible: responsable
rest (=remains): le reste
  (=others): les autres
to rest: se reposer
restaurant: le restaurant
return: le retour
to return: retourner; revenir;
  rentrer
return ticket: le billet aller et
  retour
rich: riche
to get rid (of): se débarrasser
  (de)
right: droit
on the right: à droite
to be right: avoir raison

that's right: c'est ça
to ring: sonner; téléphoner
risk: le risque
river: la rivière; le fleuve
road: le chemin; la route
to rob: voler
roll: le petit pain
roof: le toit
room: la salle; la pièce; la
  chambre
      (=space): la place
round (adj.): rond
      (prep.): autour (de)
to run: courir
to run away: se sauver
to run up: monter en courant
Russia: la Russie
Russian: russe

sad: triste
salt: le sel
same: même
sand: la sable
satisfied: satisfait
saucepan: la casserole
saucer: la soucoupe
sausage: le saucisson
to save: sauver
to say: dire
scarcely: à peine
Scotland: l'Écosse (f)
Scottish: écossais
sea: la mer
to search (someone): fouiller
  (quelqu'un)
       (for): chercher
seat (e.g. in train): la place
seated: assis
second (=time): la seconde

second (adj.): deuxième;
  second
secret: secret (ète)
secretary: le (la) secrétaire
to see: voir
to seem: sembler: paraître;
  avoir l'air (de)
to seize: saisir
seldom: rarement
to sell: vendre
to send: envoyer
sense: le sens
sentence: la phrase
separate: séparé; à part
serious: sérieux (-se); grave
to set (of sun): se coucher
to serve: servir
service: le service
to settle (bill): régler (le
  compte)
several: plusieurs
to sew: coudre
shadow: l'ombre (f)
to shake: secouer
to shake someone's hand:
  serrer la main à quelqu'un
what a shame!: quel dommage!
to shave: (se) raser
sheep: le mouton
shelf: le rayon
to shine: briller
shoe: la chaussure; le soulier
to shoot: tirer; fusiller
shop: le magasin; la boutique
short: court
shoulder: une épaule
shout: le cri
to shout: crier
to show: montrer

to shut: fermer
to shut in: enfermer
shutter: le volet
sick: malade
to be sick: vomir; dégueuler
  (sl.)
side: le côté
on one side . . . the other:
  d'un côté . . . de l'autre côté
by the side of: au bord de
to signal: faire signe (à)
since (time): depuis
to sing: chanter
single ticket: le billet simple
sister: la soeur
to sit (down): s'asseoir
to be sitting: être assis(e)
situated (at): situé (à)
sky: le ciel
sleep: le sommeil
to sleep: dormir
to go to sleep: s'endormir
slice: la tranche
to slide: glisser
slight: léger (-ère)
slightly: un peu
slightest: le (la) moindre
to slip: glisser
slipper: la pantoufle
slow (-ly): lent (lentement)
to slow down: ralentir
small: petit
to smash: casser; briser
to smile: sourire
smile: le sourire
to smoke: fumer
snow: la neige
to snow: neiger
so: si (=therefore): donc

so much/many: tant (de)
so (very): tellement
soaked: trempé
soft; softly: doux (-ce);
  doucement
soil: la terre
soldier: le soldat
some: de (+def. article)
some (pron.): en
somebody: quelqu'un
something: quelque chose
sometimes: quelquefois
somewhere: quelque part
somewhere else: ailleurs; autre
  part
son: le fils
soon: bientôt
as soon as: dès que; aussitôt
  que
as soon as possible: aussitôt
  que possible
to be sorry: regretter
sort: la sorte
sound: le bruit
south: le sud
southern: méridional (-aux)
Soviet Union: l'Union (f)
  soviétique
Spain: l'Espagne (f)
Spanish: espagnol
to speak: parler
to spend (time): passer
  (money): dépenser
in spite of: malgré
spoon: la cuiller; la cuillère
spot (=place): l'endroit (m)
  (=stain): la tache
square: la place
  (adj.): carré

stairs: l'escalier (m)

stamp: le timbre

to stamp (e.g. documents): tamponner

to stand: se tenir; (être) debout

to stand up: se lever

star: une étoile

to stare: regarder fixement

to start (doing): commencer (à); se mettre (à)

      (e.g. car): démarrer

station: la gare

to stay: rester

to steal: voler

steep: raide

step: la marche

stick: le bâton

to stick: coller

still: toujours

stomach: le ventre

stone: la pierre

to stop: s'arrêter

storm: l'orage (m)

story: l'histoire (f)

straight: droit

straight on: tout droit

strange: étrange; bizarre

street: la rue

to strike (e.g. clocks): sonner

      (=hit): frapper

      (=stop work): faire la grève

string: la ficelle

strong: fort

student: un(e) étudiant(e)

stupid: bête; stupide

to succeed (in): reussir (à)

success: le succès

such: tel (-lle)

suddenly: tout à coup; soudain

sugar: le sucre

suit: le complet

suitcase: la valise

summer: l'été (m)

sun: le soleil

sunrise (sunset): le lever (coucher) du soleil

to suppose: supposer

sure: sûr; certain

surprise: la surprise

to surprise: surprendre; étonner

surrounded (by): entouré (de)

suspicious: suspect

to sweep: balayer

sweet: le bonbon

sweet (sugary) (adj.): sucré

to swim: nager; se baigner

Switzerland: la Suisse

table: la table

table napkin: la serviette

tablet: le comprimé

to take: prendre

to take (a person): mener

      (=carry): porter

to take away (person): emmener

      (thing): emporter

to take off: ôter; enlever; (aeroplanes) décoller

to take out: sortir

to take up: monter

tall: (people) grand; (things) haut

tap: le robinet

task: la tâche

tax (income): les impôts (m)
tea: le thé
to teach: enseigner; apprendre
  (à)
teacher: le prof(esseur)
to telephone: téléphoner
television: la télé(vision)
to tell: dire
      (=recount): raconter
tennis: le tennis
terrible: terrible; affreux(-se)
to thank: remercier
thanks (a lot): merci
  (beaucoup)
theatre: le théâtre
then: puis; alors
there: là; y
over there: là-bas
there is (are): voilà
therefore: donc
thick: épais (-sse)
thief: le voleur
thin: maigre
thing: la chose
to think: penser; réfléchir; croire
a third: un tiers
thirst: la soif
to be thirsty: avoir soif
though: bien que; quoique
  (+ subj.)
as though: comme si
thousand: mille
to throw: jeter
thus: ainsi
ticket: le billet
tie: la cravate
till: jusqu'à ce que (+ subj.)
time: le temps; (by the clock)
  l'heure (f); (occasion) la fois

timetable: un horaire
tin: la boîte
tip: le pourboire
tired: fatigué
tiring: fatigant
tobacco: le tabac
tobacconist's shop: le tabac
today: aujourd'hui
together: ensemble
tomato: la tomate
tomorrow: demain
too (=also): aussi
too (much): trop
tooth: le dent
top: le haut
to touch: toucher
tourist: le (la) touriste
towards: vers
towel: la serviette
tower: la tour
town: la ville
Town Hall: l'Hôtel (m) de
  Ville
traffic: la circulation
train: le train
to travel: voyager
traveller: le voyageur
tree: l'arbre (m)
trip (excursion): la promenade
trousers: le pantalon
true: vrai
truth: la vérité
to try (to): essayer (de)
turn: le tour
to turn: tourner
to turn round: faire demi-tour
typist: la dactylo(graphe)

umbrella: le parapluie

uncle: un oncle
under: sous
to understand: comprendre
to undress: se déshabiller
unfortunately: malheureusement
unhappy: malheureux (-se)
United States: les États-Unis
  (m)
unpleasant: désagreable
until (conj.): jusqu'à ce que
  (+subj.)
unwell: souffrant; malade
upon: sur
to use: employer; se servir
  (de)
usually: d'habitude;
  normalement

to vanish: disparaître
Venice: Venise
very: très
village: le village
visit: la visite
to visit: visiter
voice: la voix

to wait for: attendre
waiting-room: la salle d'attente
waitress: la serveuse
to wake up: (se) réveiller
walk: la promenade
to walk: marcher
to go for a walk: se promener
wall: le mur
wallet: le portefeuille
to want: vouloir; désirer
warm: chaud
to wash: (se) laver
to wash up: faire la vaisselle

washing (=clothes): le linge
to waste: gaspiller
watch: la montre
to watch: regarder
water: l'eau (f)
way (=road): le chemin
  (=manner): la manière; la
    façon
way out: la sortie
to wear: porter
weather: le temps
week: la semaine
weekend: le weekend
weight: le poids
to welcome: accueillir
well: bien; eh bien!
west: l'ouest (m)
wet: mouillé
when: quand; lorsque
(steering) wheel: le volant
where: où
whereas: tandis que
while: pendant que; tandis que
to whisper: chuchoter
white: blanc (-che)
whole: entier (-ière)
why: pourquoi
wide: large
widow: la veuve
wife: la femme
willingly: volontiers
to win: gagner
wind: le vent
window: la fenêtre
wine: le vin
winter: l'hiver (m)
to wipe: essuyer
to wish: vouloir; désirer
with: avec

without: sans
woman: la femme
wonderful: merveilleux (-se)
wood: le bois
word: le mot
work: le travail
to work: travailler
workman (woman): un(e)
  ouvrier (-ère)
to worry: (s') inquiéter
worse: pire
to write: écrire

to be wrong: avoir tort; se
  tromper (de)

year: un an; une année
yellow: jaune
yes: oui; si
yesterday: hier
yesterday evening: hier soir
yet: encore; pourtant
young: jeune

to zig-zag: zigzaguer